The Albemarle Library for Schools

ASPECTS OF SCIENCE FICTION

Aspects of Science Fiction

EDITED BY

G. D. DOHERTY, B.A.

Senior English Master,
Poundswick Grammar School, Manchester

JOHN MURRAY
50 ALBEMARLE STREET
LONDON

1533

© G. D. Doherty 1959

Printed in Great Britain by
Billing and Sons Ltd., Guildford and London

CONTENTS

ACKNOWLEDGMENTS

THANKS are due to the following authors (or their representatives) who have kindly permitted the reproduction of copyright material.

The author for 'Pictures Don't Lie' by Katherine McLean.

The author for 'He Walked Around the Horses' by H. Beam Piper.

The author for 'The Cold Equations' by Tom Godwin.

The author, Messrs. Hart-Davis Ltd. and Harold Matson Company (Canada) for 'A Sound of Thunder' from *Golden Apples of the Sun* by Ray Bradbury.

The above and Love Romances Publishing Co. Inc. for 'Zero Hour' from *The Illustrated Man* by Ray Bradbury.

The executors of H. G. Wells for 'The Crystal Egg' from *Tales of Space and Time* and 'The Sea Raiders' from *The Plattner Story and Others*.

The author, Messrs. Eyre and Spottiswoode and Messrs. Farrar, Straus and Cudahy Inc. (Canada) for 'Dormant' by A. E. Van Vogt.

The authors and Messrs. Faber & Faber Ltd. for 'Dumb Show' and 'Panel Game' from *Space, Time and Nathaniel* by Brian W. Aldiss and 'The Nine Billion Names of God' by Arthur C. Clarke from *Best SF Two*.

The author, Messrs. John Lane (Bodley Head) Ltd. and Messrs. McClelland and Stewart Ltd. (Canada) for 'The Man in Asbestos' from *Nonsense Novels* by Stephen Leacock.

G. D. D.

INTRODUCTION

O star (the fairest one in sight),
We grant your loftiness the right
To some obscurity . . .
(Robert Frost, *Choose Something Like a Star.*)

SCIENCE FICTION (known to its devotees as SF) is a difficult term to define because it covers such a wide variety of
themes and ideas. Its literary quality ranges from the third-
rate to imaginative writing of a very high standard indeed.
Stories about space ships, interplanetary warfare or time-
travel have a frankly popular appeal, so that for many
years they were regarded by serious readers as an inferior
species of writing—'Super-Westerns' in which the cowboys
and Indians had been replaced by Earthmen and Martians.
Of course, there was, and still is, some truth in this accusa-
tion. Many of the cheap magazines and novelettes whose
lurid covers sensationally depict bug-eyed monsters or
pseudo-scientific machinery deserve this contempt. We do
not, however, condemn all novelists because there are many
bad ones; and in recent years SF has been widely, though
often grudgingly, accepted as a serious and intelligent form
of literature.

Since then, readers have discovered that SF has an interesting and honourable history, and that, like most 'new'
creations, people have known about it for a long time.
Lucian of Samosata wrote an interesting account of a journey to the moon as long ago as the second century A.D.
and many writers after him used the idea of a lunar visit,
or some other fabulous journey, for humorous or satirical
purposes. *Gulliver's Travels* would certainly be accepted as
SF, not to mention passages from books like *Cyrano de*

Bergerac, or *Dr. Jekyll and Mr. Hyde*. During the latter half
of the nineteenth century SF became firmly established as
an immensely popular kind of fiction by the brilliantly
prophetic stories of Jules Verne. He was followed by 'the
grand old man' of SF, H. G. Wells, in whose stories can be
found practically all the themes which interest writers today. Indeed, had all the novels and stories which followed
H. G. Wells' books been of equal calibre, there would have
been no need to reinstate SF as literature.

Before considering these particular themes, we must try
to discover what it is that gives SF its special character
and distinguishes it from other kinds of writing. The
ordinary novelist is usually interested in people and his
main aim is to reveal their personalities through their
actions. Regarding such an attitude as a criterion of literary
merit, many critics attack SF, because they find it deficient
in good characterization. They fail to understand, however,
the intention of SF writers, who are not concerned with
the particular lives and conflicts of individuals so much
as with mankind in general and man's position in the Universe. Thus the men and women who appear in these stories
are mere representatives of humanity, and it is the environment which surrounds them, or the problems arising
from it which usually inspires the SF story. The Universe
is greater than man—or any other creature which may be
striving for mastery over Nature; the struggle for progress
or supremacy may involve forces entirely beyond mankind's control or comprehension; the scientist does not
appreciate the full implications of what he is doing—these
and similar convictions are at the core of many apparently
very different SF stories, *The Nine Billion Names of God*
and *A Sound of Thunder*, for instance. Thus it is the sense
of disquiet, the knowledge that mankind is only a small
part of an infinitely greater order, which gives SF its characteristic flavour.

Not all the events of these stories take place on a large
scale, nor is there always an open conflict. *The Crystal Egg*,

for instance, merely describes the features of a distant world, while in *The Man in Asbestos* we are shown, very humorously, some of the dangers inherent in superficial ideas of progress. The SF writer is interested in every aspect of human development, immediately likely or remotely possible, and in every imaginable facet of the strange universe in which we live. 'Everything is unlikely if we consider coolly,' says Brian Aldiss, 'the stars, the fingernails.' At the heart of almost every SF story there is a problem or a hypothesis born of this sense of wonder. The rather clever speculation which inspired, for example, *The Nine Billion Names of God* is easily discerned; in *The Cold Equations*, the central problem is not so obvious, although it is there and suggested in the title. The sources of inspiration are not always confined to science in a narrow sense either, for developments in society can be just as interesting as developments in the laboratory.

It is easier, of course, for a fiction writer to make the happiness or suffering of one individual more interesting or important to us than the destruction of a distant world; nevertheless the SF writer can offer other satisfactions. His subject is the unknown, he has ample opportunity to create suspense, excitement, a sense of adventure. Most important of all, perhaps, the many themes of SF are inspired by the most breathtaking and awe-inspiring elements of our own technological civilization. The sciences of chemistry, biochemistry, biology, physics, engineering, astronomy (to name only the most obvious) have captured the popular imagination with the immense strides they have made in the twentieth century. That is why the SF writer has the opportunity of reaching a much larger audience than many other serious authors.

For this reason there are many scientists who write SF in the hope of giving a wide public some knowledge of important developments in science. They take this aspect of their writing very seriously and would like to see more stories concerned with immediately likely developments, based on a sound knowledge of scientific principles and techniques. They see SF as a convenient way of popularizing science and therefore they disapprove of stories of a depressing or fantastic nature. This attitude, however, is too narrow, and many of the best SF writers are very critical of material advancement which places terrible powers in the hands of morally irresponsible mankind. They continually attack the shallow conception that more TV sets, more electric washers, motor cars or space ships can really make us any happier.

SOME OF THE MAJOR THEMES OF SF

Despite the variety and complexity of SF stories it is possible to recognize certain dominant themes. Some of these involve knowledge and ideas, particularly about space travel, which are used so frequently that they are now taken for granted by the SF writer and reader. They are 'the rules of the game,' forming a background against which the story takes place.

Inevitably, perhaps, this has led to the growth of a jargon in which terms like android, esp-men, hyper-space, blast-off, need no explanation to the devotee, but are sometimes gibberish to new readers. For these a glossary of the more common SF words and phrases has been placed at the end of this book.

SPACE

Most people, if asked to define SF, would say, 'Oh, stories about space ships.' There is no doubt that the desire to fling off the shackles of gravity and escape to the Moon, or even further into space, has provided the inspiration for many SF stories. We know a great deal about space travel —much more, for instance, both about the Moon and how to get there, than Christopher Columbus knew about America when he sailed the Atlantic. Most writers are well acquainted with these technical details, particularly those who believe in the instructional value of SF. Arthur C. Clarke is a well-known English exponent of this type of fiction and in a novel like *Prelude to Space* almost all the interest is of a documentary kind.

Stories in which the technicalities of space flight provide the sole interest are uncommon, however; more frequently space and space ships provide the background, which must, within the limits of our knowledge, be accurately drawn. In *The Cold Equations* the space ship is an instrument of fate, an agent of the mathematical laws by which the girl is doomed. Similarly, in *Pictures Don't Lie*, although the descriptions (such as they are) of the aliens' ship are technically credible, the interest is centred more on the failure of the physicist than on the nature of space flight or of the aliens.

Modern astronomy has revealed the structure of our own solar system and galaxy, and of the greater universe of which these are a part. One of the most amazing aspects of this new knowledge is the, to us, incomprehensible distances between the stars. It would take a space ship travelling at 25,000 m.p.h. about six months to reach Mars. One of the nearest stars to our sun is Procyon: it would take about twenty-two years to travel there and back at the speed of light—*i.e. 186,000 miles per second*! Thus we can say, fairly confidently, that man will never reach beyond the solar system in rocket ships. SF has devised two methods of escaping this limitation. The first is the construction of a 'star ship,' a space ship so vast that people can live, reproduce and die on board, their children reaching the stars several generations later. Secondly, some principle, of which we are as yet ignorant, is presumed to exist, by which we could travel faster than the speed of light— hence the 'hyper-space drive' which opens other galaxies to the SF reader.

TIME AND THE FOURTH DIMENSION

Ever since the publication in 1895 of H. G. Wells' story, *The*

Time Machine, time stories have been popular. They are not easy to write, however, as there are certain philosophical difficulties to be taken into account. For example, could a visit to the past affect the present (the denouement of *A Sound of Thunder* depends upon the cumulative effect of the death of a prehistoric butterfly)? Are the events of the past quite unalterable? If so, would a time-traveller be torn apart by water-drops in a rainstorm? Indeed, how could he breathe? For, if the past is really unalterable, every atom of every molecule has its fixed place which could never give way to the traveller or his machine. Again, is the future predestined, so that even foreknowledge would not help us to avoid an evil fate? Considerations like these form problems to which many SF stories provide intriguing answers.

Furthermore, with the development of modern physics, we are no longer sure what is meant by matter, space or time. There are good grounds for believing that if you set out in a space ship for the Moon, and travelled faster than light, you would return before you had started!

> There was a young lady named Bright
> Who travelled much faster than light.
>> She started one day,
>> In a relative way,
> And returned on the previous night.

So wrote a wit who had been trying to understand Einstein's Theory of Relativity. If we could travel as fast as this, we could move in another dimension—in time as well as in space.

If there could be a Fourth Dimension, why not a fifth or sixth, with different worlds existing simultaneously in different 'times', but in the same space? Fascinating and difficult conjectures such as these often provide the theme of a story like *He Walked Around the Horses* or the background for a story like *Zero Hour*.

INVASION

In fact, *Zero Hour*, although involving the existence of a Fourth Dimension, is really a story about an alien invasion of Earth. The method is novel, and depends upon special qualities of mind possessed by children but which adults have lost. In the hands of a good author, whose writing is exciting without becoming crudely sensational, this theme will always produce a good story. At the same time it provides ample opportunity for comment on the inadequacies of over-confident humanity.

H. G. Wells' *The War of the Worlds* published in 1898, was the first of many outstanding stories which have been written on this theme.

OTHER WORLDS

The opposite idea—man's attempt to reach and conquer other worlds—is equally popular. In these stories the author must rely to a great extent upon his imagination; indeed, the mere description of an imaginary world set in a plot with the minimum of action can provide a moving and interesting story (*The Crystal Egg*). More often man is found attempting to adapt himself to new surroundings, or in conflict with alien creatures, or discovering more about his own nature in some distant outpost of the Galaxy.

To enjoy SF we must accept the existence of other planets capable of supporting human life. There is no space here to discuss the mathematical probabilities of mankind's making such discoveries, but there is at least one group of eminent astronomers who believe that there may be about 1,000,000 planets in our Galaxy alone that could support life. Accepting this possibility, we must also accept the possibility of alien creatures who have achieved a standard of science and technology equal or superior to our own. The Galaxy has existed for a very long time, and some of its mysteries may affect the Earth. Here you find the inspiration for a sinister story like *Dormant*.

REALISM

In complete contrast there are those writers who, far from allowing their fancy full flight, confine themselves to the prediction and description of developments likely in the near future. They write in a very 'realistic' manner and describe their scenes in accurate detail which can be worked up, for the most part, from a knowledge of present-day techniques. *The Sea Raiders* is a good example of this. The appearances of the monsters are well documented; their entirely credible physical shape is minutely described; as some form of octopus or squid they are given an appropriate zoological name. These factors, together with a very straightforward style of writing, create an illusion of reality.

This could almost be described as a 'school' of SF as its exponents disapprove of fantasy and refer to those who describe interplanetary war, or some other fearful disaster, as the 'Gloom School.' They are popularizers rather than poets who can write of rocketry, atomics, medicine, radio, astronomy, with considerable authority. Some authors, like H. G. Wells or Arthur C. Clarke, handle either style with equal ease and ability.

WARFARE

The devastation of the world by nuclear war is such an obvious theme that many of the better writers avoid it altogether. It allows a great deal of opportunity for the elaboration of the most gruesome aspects of radiation, or for the most morbid flights of fancy, and many unscrupulous writers are guilty of pursuing these horrors for their own sake. This is not to say that good accounts of warfare in the future have not been written. *Dumb Show* is a moving story which should remind us that scientists can devise other weapons equally as devastating as the H Bomb.

Catastrophe

There are many natural catastrophes other than war which could affect mankind. This is a favourite theme of such stories as *In the Days of the Comet* by H. G. Wells, *The Black Cloud* by Fred Hoyle, or *The Death of Grass* by John Christopher.

Disaster caused by man's foolishness is hinted at in *The Day of the Triffids* by John Wyndham. *The Nine Billion Names of God* contains a similar thought, though it is conceit rather than foolishness which is the fatal weakness of the Western scientists in this story.

The World of Tomorrow

As distinct from those who are absorbed in the future destruction of mankind by some natural or man-made disasters, there have always been thinkers trying to predict what the 'world of tomorrow' will be like. For the most part their books have depicted 'perfect' societies freed from the pointless frustrations of their own day, where men and women, unhampered by the shackles of useless convention and no longer oppressed by laws which discriminate between rich and poor, can grow into full maturity of mind and body. An imaginary society of this kind, usually quite improbable and impractical, is called a 'Utopia' (from the Greek word meaning 'nowhere').

The earliest Utopia in European literature is Plato's *Republic*, written during the third century B.C. Countless others have followed, and there is a clear tendency for some SF writers to produce stories particularly concerned with the development of society. The most interesting characteristic of the SF 'Utopia' is that in contrast with its optimistic forerunners, it nearly always seems to us a very unpleasant place even though it satisfies its own inhabitants. Twentieth century science and society have, it seems, disillusioned the modern writer.

Plenty of space is needed to elaborate a Utopia, so the

best examples are found in full-length novels like *Farenheit 451* by Ray Bradbury, *1984* by George Orwell or *Brave New World* by Aldous Huxley. In this anthology *Panel Game* with its satirical picture of a neurotic society dominated by the TV screen is not very far from the world of Orwell's *1984*.

HUMOUR

SF writers do not belong only to schools of 'Gloom' or 'Realism.' There are humorous stories dealing with most of the SF themes which have been discussed. *The Man in Asbestos*, despite its serious undertones, is an early and very amusing parody of *The Time Machine*. The SF humorist is always ready to poke fun at human beings who, despite their scientific achievements, find themselves in very undignified situations. Indeed, SF lends itself naturally to satire, through which we are laughed into a realization of our own folly and shortcomings.

From this brief analysis of the main themes of SF it should be clear that science in its narrow sense often provides simply the background for the main events of a story. Nevertheless, a writer will fail to convince us if his facts are inaccurate, or if he has no knowledge of SF conventions. That is why most efforts to write a 'story about space ships' fall so woefully short of the mark.

Finally, all good SF stories demand some serious thought from the reader. The problems presented, though not always easy to grasp, are usually concerned with man in his relation to the Universe around him; to appreciate them the reader must have some intelligent views about himself and the world he lives in; that is why SF commands respect as a serious branch of literature even when it is written to make us laugh.

G. D. DOHERTY

PICTURES DON'T LIE

KATHERINE MACLEAN

THE MAN from the *News* asked, 'What do you think of the aliens, Mr. Nathen? Are they friendly? Do they look human?'

'Very human,' said the thin young man.

Outside, rain sleeted across the big windows with a steady, faint drumming, blurring and dimming the view of the airfield where *They* would arrive. On the concrete runways the puddles were pockmarked with rain, and the grass growing untouched between the runways of the unused field glistened wetly, bending before gusts of wind.

Back at a respectful distance from the place where the huge space ship would land were the grey shapes of trucks, where TV camera crews huddled inside their mobile units, waiting. Farther back in the deserted, sandy landscape, between distant sandy hills, artillery was ringed in a great circle, and in the distance across the horizon bombers stood ready at airfields, guarding the world against possible treachery from the first alien ship ever to land from space.

'Do you know anything about their home planet?' asked the man from the *Herald*.

The *Times* man stood with the others, listening absently, thinking of questions but reserving them. Joseph R. Nathen, the thin young man with the straight black hair and the tired lines on his face, was being treated with respect by his interviewers. He was obviously on edge, and they did

11

not want to harry him with too many questions at once.
They wanted to keep his good will. Tomorrow he would
be one of the biggest celebrities ever to appear in headlines.

'No, nothing directly.'

'Any ideas or deductions?' the *Herald* persisted.

'Their world must be Earthlike to them,' the weary-
looking young man answered uncertainly. 'The environment evolves the animal. But only in relative terms, of
course.' He looked at them with a quick glance and then
looked away evasively, his lank black hair beginning to
cling to his forehead with sweat. 'That doesn't necessarily
mean anything.'

'Earthlike,' muttered a reporter, writing it down as if he
had noticed nothing more in the reply.

The *Times* man glanced at the *Herald*, wondering if he
had noticed, and received a quick glance in exchange.

The *Herald* asked Nathen, 'You think they are dangerous,
then?'

It was the kind of question, assuming much, that usually
broke reticence and brought forth quick facts—when it hit
the mark. They all knew of the military precautions,
although they were not supposed to know.

The question missed. Nathen glanced out the window
vaguely. 'No, I wouldn't say so.'

'You think they are friendly, then?' said the *Herald*,
equally positive on the opposite tack.

A fleeting smile touched Nathen's lips. 'Those I know
are.'

There was no lead in this direction, and they had to get
the basic facts of the story before the ship came. The
Times asked, 'What led up to your contacting them?'

Nathen answered, after a hesitation, 'Static. Radio static.
The Army told you my job, didn't they?'

The Army had told them nothing at all. The officer who
had conducted them in for the interview stood glowering
watchfully, as if he objected by instinct to telling anything
to the public.

Nathen glanced at him doubtfully. 'My job is radio de-coder for the Department of Military Intelligence. I use a directional pick-up, tune in on foreign bands, record any scrambled or coded messages I hear, and build automatic decoders and descramblers for all the basic scramble patterns.'

The officer cleared his throat but said nothing.

The reporters smiled, noting that down.

Security regulations had changed since arms inspection had been legalized by the U.N. Complete information being the only public security against secret rearmament, spying and prying had come to seem a public service. Its aura had changed. It was good public relations to admit to it.

Nathen continued, 'In my spare time I started directing the pick-up at stars. There's radio noise from stars, you know. Just stuff that sounds like spatter static, and an occasional squawk. People have been listening to it for a long time, and researching, trying to work out why stellar radiation on those bands comes in such jagged bursts. It didn't seem natural.'

He paused and smiled uncertainly, aware that the next thing he would say was the thing that would make him famous—an idea that had come to him while he listened, an idea as simple and as perfect as the one that came to Newton when he saw the apple fall.

'I decided it wasn't natural. I tried decoding it.'

Hurriedly, he tried to explain it away and make it seem obvious. 'You see, there's an old intelligence trick, speeding up a message on a record until it sounds just like that, a short squawk of static, and then broadcasting it. Under-grounds use it. I'd heard that kind of screech before.'

'You mean they broadcast at us in code?' asked the News.

'It's not exactly code. All you need to do is record it and slow it down. They're not broadcasting at us. If a star has planets, inhabited planets, and there is broadcasting be-tween them, they would send it on a tight beam to save power.' He looked for comprehension. 'You know, like a spotlight. Theoretically, a tight beam can go on for ever without losing power. But aiming would be difficult from planet to planet. You can't expect a beam to stay on target, over such distances, more than a few seconds at a time. So they'd naturally compress each message into a short half-second- or one-second-length package and send it a few hundred times in one long blast to make sure it is picked up during the instant the beam swings across the target.'

He was talking slowly and carefully, remembering that this explanation was for the newspapers. 'When a stray beam swings through our section of space, there's a sharp peak in noise level from that direction. The beams are swinging to follow their own planets at home, and the distance between there and here exaggerates the speed of swing tremendously, so we wouldn't pick up more than a *bip* as it passes.'

'How did you account for the number of squawks coming in?' the *Times* asked. 'Do stellar systems rotate on the plane of the Galaxy?' It was a private question; he spoke impulsively from interest and excitement.

The radio decoder grinned, the lines of strain vanishing from his face for a moment. 'Maybe we're intercepting everybody's telephone calls, and the whole Galaxy is swarming with races that spend all day yacking at each other over the radio. Maybe the human type is standard model.'

'It would take something like that,' the *Times* agreed. They smiled at each other.

The *News* asked, 'How did you happen to pick up television instead of voices?'

'Not by accident,' Nathen explained patiently. 'I'd recognized a scanning pattern, and I wanted pictures. Pictures are understandable in any language.'

Near the interviewers, a senator paced back and forth,

muttering his memorized speech of welcome and nervously glancing out of the wide, streaming windows into the grey sleeting rain.

Opposite the windows of the long room was a small raised platform flanked by the tall shapes of TV cameras and sound pick-ups on booms, and darkened floodlights, arranged and ready for the senator to make his speech of welcome to the aliens and the world. A shabby radio sending set stood beside it without a case to conceal its parts, two cathode television tubes flickering nakedly on one side and the speaker humming on the other. A vertical panel of dials and knobs jutted up before them, and a small hand-mike sat ready on the table before the panel. It was connected to a box-like, expensively-cased piece of equipment with 'Radio Lab, U.S. Property' stencilled on it.

'I recorded a couple of package screeches from Sagittarius and began working on them,' Nathen added. 'It took a couple of months to find the synchronizing signals and set the scanners close enough to the right time to even get a pattern. When I showed the pattern to the Department, they gave me full time to work on it, and an assistant to help. It took eight months to pick out the colour bands and assign them the right colours, to get anything intelligible on the screen.'

The shabby-looking mess of exposed parts was the original receiver that they had laboured over for ten months, adjusting and re-adjusting to reduce the maddening rippling plaids of unsynchronized colour scanners to some kind of sane picture.

'Trial and error,' said Nathan, 'but it came out all right. The wide band spread of the squawks had suggested colour TV from the beginning.'

He walked over and touched the set. The speaker bipped slightly and the grey screen flickered with a flash of colour at the touch. The set was awake and sensitive, tuned to receive from the great interstellar space ship which now circled the atmosphere.

'We wondered why there were so many bands, but when we got the set working and started recording and playing everything that came in, we found we'd tapped something like a lending-library line. It was all fiction, plays.'

Between the pauses in Nathen's voice, the *Times* found himself unconsciously listening for the sound of roaring, swiftly-approaching rocket jets.

The *Post* asked, 'How did you contact the space ship?'

'I scanned and recorded a film copy of *The Rite of Spring*, the Disney-Stravinsky combination, and sent it back along the same line we were receiving from. Just testing. It wouldn't get there for a good number of years, if it got there at all, but I thought it would please the library to get a new record in.

'Two weeks later, when we caught and slowed a new batch of recordings, we found an answer. It was obviously meant for us. It was a flash of the Disney being played to a large audience, and then the audience sitting and waiting before a blank screen. The signal was very clear and loud. We'd intercepted a space ship. They were asking for an encore, you see. They liked the film and wanted more. . . .'

He smiled at them in sudden thought. 'You can see them for yourself. It's all right down the hall where the linguists are working on the automatic translator.'

The listening officer frowned and cleared his throat, and the thin young man turned to him quickly. 'No security reason why they should not see the broadcasts, is there? Perhaps you should show them.' He said to the reporters reassuringly, 'It's right down the hall. You will be informed the moment the space ship approaches.'

The interview was very definitely over. The lank-haired, nervous young man turned away and seated himself at the radio set while the officer swallowed his objections and showed them dourly down the hall to a closed door.

They opened it and fumbled into a darkened room crowded with empty folding chairs, dominated by a glowing bright screen. The door closed behind them, bringing total darkness.

There was the sound of reporters fumbling their way into seats around him, but the *Times* man remained standing, aware of an enormous surprise, as if he had been asleep and wakened to find himself in the wrong country.

The bright colours of the double image seemed the only real thing in the darkened room. Even blurred as they were, he could see that the action was subtly different, the shapes subtly not right.

He was looking at aliens.

The impression was of two humans disguised, humans moving oddly, half dancing, half crippled. Carefully, afraid the images would go away, he reached up to his breast-pocket, took out his polarized glasses, rotated one lens at right angles to the other, and put them on.

Immediately, the two beings came into sharp focus, real and solid, and the screen became a wide, illusively near window through which he watched them.

They were conversing with each other in a grey-walled room, discussing something with restrained excitement. The large man in the green tunic closed his purple eyes for an instant at something the other said and grimaced, making a motion with his fingers as if shoving something away from him.

Mellerdrammer.

The second, smaller, with yellowish-green eyes, stepped closer, talking more rapidly in a lower voice. The first stood very still, not trying to interrupt.

Obviously, the proposal was some advantageous treachery, and he wanted to be persuaded. The *Times* groped for a chair and sat down.

Perhaps gesture is universal; desire and aversion, a leaning forward or a leaning back, tension, relaxation. Perhaps these actors were masters. The scenes changed: a corridor, a park-like place in what he began to realize was a space ship, a lecture-room. There were others talking and working, speaking to the man in the green tunic, and never was it unclear what was happening or how they felt.

They talked a flowing language with many short vowels and shifts of pitch, and they gestured in the heat of talk, their hands moving with an odd lagging difference of motion, not slow, but somehow drifting.

He ignored the language, but after a time the difference in motion began to arouse his interest. Something in the way they walked . . .

With an effort he pulled his mind from the plot and forced his attention to the physical difference. Brown hair in short, silky crew cuts, varied eye colours, the colours showing clearly because their irises were very large, their round eyes set very widely apart in tapering, light-brown faces. Their necks and shoulders were thick in a way that would indicate unusual strength for a human, but their wrists were narrow and their fingers long and thin and delicate.

There seemed to be more than the usual number of fingers.

Since he came in, a machine had been whirring and a voice muttering beside him. He turned from counting their fingers and looked around. Beside him sat an alert-looking man wearing earphones, watching and listening with hawk-like concentration. Beside him was a tall streamlined box. From the screen came the sound of the alien language. The man abruptly flipped a switch on the box, muttered a word into a small hand microphone, and flipped the switch back with nervous rapidity.

He reminded the *Times* man of the earphoned interpreters at the U.N. The machine was probably a vocal translator and the mutterer a linguist adding to its vocabulary. Near the screen were two other linguists taking notes.

The *Times* remembered the senator pacing in the observatory room, rehearsing his speech of welcome. The speech would not be just the empty pompous gesture he had expected. It would be translated mechanically and understood by the aliens.

On the other side of the glowing window that was the stereo screen the large protagonist in the green tunic was speaking to a pilot in a grey uniform. They stood in a brightly-lit canary-yellow control room in a space ship.

The *Times* tried to pick up the thread of the plot. Already he was interested in the fate of the hero and liked him. That was the effect of good acting, probably, for part of the art of acting is to win affection from the audience, and this actor might be the matinée idol of whole Solar Systems.

Controlled tension, betraying itself by a jerk of the hands, a too quick answer to a question. The uniformed one, not suspicious, turned his back, busying himself at some task involving a map lit with glowing red points, his motions sharing the same fluid, dragging grace of the others, as if they were under water or on a slow-motion film. The other was watching a switch set into a panel, moving closer to it, talking casually—background music coming and rising in thin chords of tension.

There was a close-up of the alien's face watching the switch, and the *Times* noted that his ears were symmetrical half-circles, almost perfect, with no earholes visible. The voice of the uniformed one answered—a brief word in a preoccupied, deep voice. His back was still turned. The other glanced at the switch, moving closer to it, talking casually, the switch coming closer and closer stereoscopically. It was in reach, filling the screen. His hand came into view, darted out, closed over the switch——

There was a sharp clap of sound and his hand opened in a frozen shape of pain. Beyond him, as his gaze swung up, stood the figure of the uniformed officer, unmoving, a weapon rigid in his hand, in the startled position in which he had turned and fired, watching with widening eyes as the man in the green tunic swayed and fell.

The tableau held, the uniformed one drooping, looking down at his hand holding the weapon which had killed, and music began to build in from the background. Just for an instant, the room and the things within it flashed into one of those bewildering colour changes that were the bane of colour television—to a colour negative of itself, a green man standing in a violet control-room, looking down at the body of a green man in a red tunic. It held for less than a second; then the colour-band alternator fell back into phase and the colours reversed to normal.

Another uniformed man came and took the weapon from the limp hand of the other, who began to explain dejectedly in a low voice while the music mounted and covered his words and the screen slowly went blank, like a window that slowly filmed over with grey fog.

The music faded.

In the dark, someone clapped appreciatively.

The earphoned man beside the *Times* shifted his earphones back from his ears and spoke briskly. 'I can't get any more. Either of you want a replay?'

There was a short silence until the linguist nearest the set said, 'I guess we've squeezed that one dry. Let's run the tape where Nathen and that ship radio boy are kidding around CQing and tuning their beams in closer. I have a hunch the boy is talking routine ham talk and giving the old radio count—one-two-three-testing.'

There was some fumbling in the semi-dark and then the screen came to life again.

It showed a flash of an audience sitting before a screen and gave a clipped chord of some familiar symphony. 'Crazy about Stravinsky and Mozart,' remarked the earphoned linguist to the *Times*, re-settling his earphones. 'Can't stand Gershwin. Can you beat that?' He turned his attention back to the screen as the right sequence came on.

The *Post*, who was sitting just in front of him, turned to the *Times* and said, 'Funny how much they look like people.' He was writing, making notes to telephone his report. 'What colour hair did that character have?'

'I didn't notice.' He wondered if he should remind the

reporter that Nathen had said he assigned the colour bands on guess, choosing the colours that gave the most plausible images. The guests, when they arrived, would turn out to be bright green with blue hair. Only the gradations of colour in the picture were sure, only the similarities and contrasts, the relationship of one colour to another.

From the screen came the sound of the alien language again. This race averaged deeper voices than human. He liked deep voices. Could he write that?

No, there was something wrong with that, too. How had Nathen established the right sound-track pitch? Was it a matter of taking the modulation as it came in, or some sort of heterodyning up and down by trial and error? Probably.

It might be safer to assume that Nathen had simply preferred deep voices.

As he sat there, doubting, an uneasiness he had seen in Nathen came back to add to his own uncertainty, and he remembered just how close that uneasiness had come to something that looked like restrained fear.

'What I don't get is why he went to all the trouble of picking up TV shows instead of just contacting them,' the *News* complained. 'They're good shows, but what's the point?'

'Maybe so we'd get to learn their language, too,' said the *Herald*.

On the screen now was the obviously unstaged and genuine scene of a young alien working over a bank of apparatus. He turned and waved and opened his mouth in the comical O shape which the *Times* was beginning to recognize as their equivalent of a smile, then went back to trying to explain something about the equipment, in elaborate, awkward gestures and carefully mouthed words.

The *Times* got up quietly, went out into the bright white stone corridor, and walked back the way he had come, thoughtfully folding his stereo glasses and putting them away.

No one stopped him. Secrecy restrictions were ambiguous here. The reticence of the Army seemed more a matter of habit—mere reflex, from the fact that it had all originated in the Intelligence Department—than any reasoned policy of keeping the landing a secret.

The main room was more crowded than he had left it. The TV camera and sound crew stood near their apparatus, the senator had found a chair and was reading, and at the far end of the room eight men were grouped in a circle of chairs, arguing something with impassioned concentration. The *Times* recognized a few he knew personally, eminent names in science, workers in field theory.

A stray phrase reached him : '—reference to the universal constants as ratio——' It was probably a discussion of ways of converting formulas from one mathematics to another for a rapid exchange of information.

They had reason to be intent, aware of the flood of insights that novel viewpoints could bring, if they could grasp them. He would have liked to go over and listen, but there was too little time left before the space ship was due, and he had a question to ask.

The hand-rigged transceiver was still humming, tuned to the sending band of the circling ship, and the young man who had started it all was sitting on the edge of the TV platform with his chin resting in one hand. He did not look up as the *Times* approached, but it was the indifference of preoccupation, not discourtesy.

The *Times* sat down on the edge of the platform beside him and took out a packet of cigarettes, then remembered the coming TV broadcast and the ban on smoking. He put them away, thoughtfully watching the diminishing rain spray against the streaming windows.

'What's wrong?' he asked.

Nathen showed that he was aware and friendly by a slight motion of his head.

'*You* tell me.'

'Hunch,' said the *Times* man. 'Sheer hunch. Everything sailing along too smoothly, everyone taking too much for granted.'

Nathen relaxed slightly. 'I'm still listening.'

'Something about the way they move . . .'

Nathen shifted to glance at him.

'That's bothered me, too.'

'Are you sure they're adjusted to the right speed?'

Nathen clenched his hands out in front of him and looked at them consideringly. 'I don't know. When I turn the tape faster, they're all rushing, and you begin to wonder why their clothes don't stream behind them, why the doors close so quickly and yet you can't hear them slam, why things fall so fast. If I turn it slower, they all seem to be swimming.' He gave the *Times* a considering sideways glance. 'Didn't catch the name.'

Country-bred guy, thought the *Times*. 'Jacob Luke, *Times*,' he said, extending his hand.

Nathen gave the hand a quick, hard grip, identifying the name. 'Sunday Science Section editor. I read it. Surprised to meet you here.'

'Likewise.' The *Times* smiled. 'Look, have you gone into this rationally, with formulas?' He found a pencil in his pocket. 'Obviously, there's something wrong with our judgment of their weight-to-speed-to-momentum ratio. Maybe it's something simple, like low gravity aboard ship, with magnetic shoes. Maybe they *are* floating slightly.'

'Why worry?' Nathen cut in. 'I don't see any reason to try to figure it out now.' He laughed and shoved back his black hair nervously. 'We'll see them in twenty minutes.'

'Will we?' asked the *Times* slowly.

There was a silence while the senator turned a page of his magazine with a slight crackling of paper and the scientists argued at the other end of the room. Nathen pushed at his lank black hair again, as if it were trying to fall forward in front of his eyes and keep him from seeing.

'Sure.' The young man laughed suddenly, talked rapidly. 'Sure we'll see them. Why shouldn't we, with all the government ready with welcome speeches, the whole Army turned out and hiding over the hill, reporters all around, newsreel cameras—everything set up to broadcast the landing to the world. The President himself shaking hands with me and waiting in Washington——'

He came to the truth without pausing for breath.

He said, 'Hell, no, they won't get here. There's some mistake somewhere. Something's wrong. I should have told the brass hats yesterday when I started adding it up. Don't know why I didn't say anything. Scared, I guess. Too much top rank around here. Lost my nerve.'

He clutched the *Times* man's sleeve. 'Look. I don't know what——'

A green light flashed on the sending-receiving set. Nathen didn't look at it, but he stopped talking.

The loud-speaker on the set broke into a voice speaking in the aliens' language. The senator started and looked nervously at it, straightening his tie. The voice stopped.

Nathen turned and looked at the loud-speaker. His worry seemed to be gone.

'What is it?' the *Times* asked anxiously.

'He says they've slowed enough to enter the atmosphere now. They'll be here in five to ten minutes, I guess. That's Bud. He's all excited. He says holy smoke, what a murky-looking planet we live on.' Nathen smiled. 'Kidding.'

The *Times* was puzzled. 'What does he mean, murky? It can't be raining over much territory on Earth.' Outside, the rain was slowing and bright-blue patches of sky were shining through breaks in the cloud blanket, glittering blue light from the drops that ran down the windows. He tried to think of an explanation. 'Maybe they're trying to land on Venus.' The thought was ridiculous, he knew. The space ship was following Nathen's sending beam. It couldn't miss Earth. 'Bud' had to be kidding.

The green light glowed on the set again, and they stopped speaking, waiting for the message to be recorded, slowed, and replayed. The cathode screen came to life suddenly with a picture of the young man sitting at his sending set, his back turned, watching a screen at one side that showed a glimpse of a huge dark plain approaching. As the ship plunged down towards it, the illusion of solidity melted into a boiling turbulence of black clouds. They expanded in an inky swirl, looked huge for an instant, and then blackness swallowed the screen. The young alien swung around to face the camera, speaking a few words as he moved, made the O of a smile again, then flipped the switch and the screen went grey.

Nathen's voice was suddenly toneless and strained. 'He said something like break out the drinks, here they come.'

'The atmosphere doesn't look like that,' the *Times* said at random, knowing he was saying something too obvious even to think about. 'Not Earth's atmosphere.'

Some people drifted up. 'What did they say?'

'Entering the atmosphere, ought to be landing in five or ten minutes,' Nathen told them.

A ripple of heightened excitement ran through the room. Camera-men began adjusting the lens angles again, turning on the mike and checking it, turning on the floodlights. The scientists rose and stood near the window, still talking. The reporters trooped in from the hall and went to the windows to watch for the great event. The three linguists came in, trundling a large wheeled box that was the mechanical translator, supervising while it was hitched into the sound-broadcasting system.

'Landing where?' the *Times* asked Nathen brutally. 'Why don't you do something?'

'Tell me what to do and I'll do it,' Nathen said quietly, not moving.

It was not sarcasm. Jacob Luke of the *Times* looked sideways at the strained whiteness of his face and moderated his tone. 'Can't you contact them?'

'Not while they're landing.'

'What now?' The *Times* took out a packet of cigarettes, remembered the rule against smoking, and put it back.

'We just wait.' Nathen leaned his elbow on one knee and his chin in his hand.

They waited.

All the people in the room were waiting. There was no more conversation. A bald man of the scientist group was automatically buffing his fingernails over and over and inspecting them without seeing them; another absently polished his glasses, held them up to the light, put them on, and then a moment later took them off and began polishing again. The television crew concentrated on their jobs, moving quietly and efficiently, with perfectionist care, minutely arranging things that did not need to be arranged, checking things that had already been checked.

This was to be one of the great moments of human history, and they were all trying to forget that fact and remain impassive and wrapped up in the problems of their jobs, as good specialists should.

After an interminable age the *Times* consulted his watch. Three minutes had passed. He tried holding his breath a moment, listening for a distant approaching thunder of jets. There was no sound.

The sun came out from behind the clouds and lit up the field like a great spotlight on an empty stage.

Abruptly, the green light shone on the set again, indicating that a squawk message had been received. The recorder recorded it, slowed it, and fed it back to the speaker. It clicked and the sound was very loud in the still, tense room.

The screen remained grey, but Bud's voice spoke a few words in the alien language. He stopped, the speaker clicked, and the light went out. When it was plain that nothing more would occur and no announcement was to be made of what was said, the people in the room turned back to the windows and talk picked up again.

Somebody told a joke and laughed alone.

One of the linguists remained turned towards the loudspeaker, then looked at the widening patches of blue sky showing out the window, his expression puzzled. He had understood.

'It's dark,' the thin Intelligence Department decoder

translated, low-voiced, to the man from the *Times*. 'Your atmosphere is *thick*. That's precisely what Bud said.'

Another three minutes. The *Times* caught himself about to light a cigarette and swore silently, blowing the match out and putting the cigarette back into its package. He listened for the sound of the rocket jets. It was time for the landing, yet he heard no blasts.

The green light came on in the transceiver.

Message in.

Instinctively, he came to his feet. Nathen abruptly was standing beside him. Then the message came in the voice he was coming to think of as Bud. It spoke and paused. Suddenly the *Times* knew.

'We've landed.' Nathen whispered the words.

The wind blew across the open spaces of white concrete and damp soil that was empty airfield, swaying the wet, shiny grass. The people in the room looked out, listening for the roar of jets, looking for the silver bulk of a space ship in the sky.

Nathen moved, seating himself at the transmitter, switching it on to warm up, checking and balancing dials. Jacob Luke of the *Times* moved softly to stand behind his right shoulder, hoping he could be useful. Nathen made a half motion of his head, as if to glance back at him, unhooked two of the earphone sets hanging on the side of the tall streamlined box that was the automatic translator, plugged them in, and handed one back over his shoulder to the *Times* man.

The voice began to come from the speaker again.

Hastily, Jacob Luke fitted the earphones over his ears. He fancied he could hear Bud's voice tremble. For a moment it was just Bud's voice speaking the alien language, and then, very distant and clear in his earphones, he heard the recorded voice of the linguist say an English word, then a mechanical click and another clear word in the voice of one of the other translators, then another as the alien's voice flowed from the loud-speaker, the cool single words

C

barely audible, overlapping and blinding like translating thought, skipping unfamiliar words yet quite astonishingly clear.

'Radar shows no buildings or civilization near. The atmosphere around us registers as thick as glue. Tremendous gas pressure, low gravity, no light at all. You didn't describe it like this. Where are you, Joe? This isn't some kind of trick, is it?' Bud hesitated, was prompted by a deeper official voice, and jerked out the words.

'If it is a trick, we are ready to repel attack.'

The linguist stood listening. He whitened slowly and beckoned the other linguist over to him and whispered to them.

Joseph Nathen looked at them with unwarranted bitter hostility while he picked up the hand mike, plugging it into the translator. 'Joe calling,' he said quietly into it in clear, slow English. 'No trick. We don't know where you are. I am trying to get a direction fix from your signal. Describe your surroundings to us if at all possible.'

Nearby, the floodlights blazed steadily on the television platform, ready for the official welcome of the aliens to Earth. The television channels of the world had been alerted to set aside their scheduled programmes for an unscheduled great event. In the long room the people waited, listened for the swelling sound of rocket jets.

This time, after the light came on, there was a long delay. The speaker sputtered and sputtered again, building to a steady scratching through which they could barely hear a dim voice. It came through in a few tinny words and then wavered back to inaudibility. The machine translated in their earphones.

'Tried . . . seemed . . . repair . . .' Suddenly it came in clearly. 'Can't tell if the auxiliary blew, too. Will try it. We might pick you up clearly on the next try. I have the volume down. Where is the landing port? Repeat. Where is the landing port? Where are you?'

Nathen put down the hand mike and carefully set a dial

on the recording box and flipped a switch, speaking over his shoulder. 'This sets it to repeat what I said the last time. It keeps repeating.' Then he sat with unnatural stillness, his head still half turned, as if he had suddenly caught a glimpse of an answer and was trying with no success whatever to grasp it.

The green warning light cut in, the recording clicked, and the play-back of Bud's face and voice appeared on the screen.

'We heard a few words, Joe, and then the receiver blew again. We're adjusting a viewing screen to pick up the long waves that go through the murk and convert them to visible light. We'll be able to see out soon. The engineer says that something is wrong with the stern jets, and the captain has had me broadcast a help call to our nearest space base.' He made the mouth O of a grin. 'The message won't reach it for some years. I trust you, Joe, but get us out of here, will you?—— They're buzzing that the screen is finally ready. Hold everything.'

The screen went grey and the green light went off.

The *Times* considered the lag required for the help call, the speaking and recording of the message just received, the time needed to reconvert a viewing screen

'They work fast.' He shifted uneasily and added at random. 'Something wrong with the time factor. All wrong. They work *too* fast.'

The green light came on again immediately. Nathen half turned to him, sliding his words hastily into the gap of time as the message was recorded and slowed. 'They're close enough for our transmission power to blow their receiver.'

If it was on Earth, why the darkness around the ship? 'Maybe they see in the high ultra-violet—the atmosphere is opaque to that band,' the *Times* suggested hastily as the speaker began to talk in the young extra-Terrestrial's voice.

That voice *was* shaking now. 'Stand by for that description.' They tensed, waiting. The *Times* brought a map of the state before his mind's eye.

'A half-circle of cliffs around the horizon. A wide muddy lake swarming with swimming things. Huge, strange white foliage all around the ship and incredibly huge, pulpy monsters attacking and eating each other on all sides. We almost landed in the lake, right on the soft edge. The mud can't hold the ship's weight, and we're sinking. The engineer says we might be able to blast free, but the tubes are mud-clogged and might blow up the ship. When can you reach us?'

The *Times* thought vaguely of the Carboniferous era. Nathen obviously had seen something he had not.

'Where are they?' the *Times* asked him quietly.

Nathen pointed to the antenna position indicators. The *Times* let his eyes follow the converging imaginary lines of focus out of the window to the sunlit airfield, the empty airfield, the drying concrete and green waving grass where the lines met.

Where the lines met. The space ship was there!

The fear of something unknown gripped him suddenly.

The space ship was broadcasting again. *'Where are you? Answer if possible! We are sinking! Where are you?'*

He saw that Nathen knew. 'What is it?' the *Times* asked hoarsely. 'Are they in another dimension or the past or on another world or what?'

Nathen was smiling bitterly, and Jacob Luke remembered that the young man had a friend in that space ship. 'My guess is that they evolved on a high-gravity planet with a thin atmosphere, near a blue-white star. Sure, they see in the ultra-violet range. Our sun is abnormally small and dim and yellow. Our atmosphere is so thick it screens our ultra-violet.' He laughed harshly. 'A good joke on us, the weird place we evolved in, the thing it did to us!'

'Where are you?' called the alien space ship. 'Hurry, please! We're sinking!'

The decoder slowed his tumbled, frightened words and looked up into *Times'* face for understanding. 'We'll rescue them,' he said quietly. 'You were right about the time factor, right about them moving at a different speed. I misunderstood. This business about squawk coding, speeding for better transmission to counteract beam waver—I was wrong.'

'What do you mean?'

'They don't speed up their broadcasts.'

'They don't——?'

Suddenly, in his mind's eye, the *Times* began to see again the play he had just seen—but the actors were moving at blurring speed, the words jerking out in a fluting, dizzying stream, thoughts and decisions passing with unfollowable rapidity, rippling faces in a twisting blur of expressions, doors slamming wildly, shatteringly, as the actors leaped in and out of rooms.

No—faster, faster—he wasn't visualizing it as rapidly as it was, an hour of talk and action in one almost instantaneous 'squawk', a narrow peak of 'noise' interfering with a single word in an Earth broadcast! Faster—faster—it was impossible. Matter could not stand such stress—inertia—momentum—abrupt weight.

It was insane. 'Why?' he asked. 'How?'

Nathen laughed again harshly, reaching for the mike. 'Get them out! There isn't a lake or river within hundreds of miles from here!'

A shiver of unreality went down the *Times*' spine. Automatically and inanely, he found himself delving in his pocket for a cigarette while he tried to grasp what had happened. 'Where are they, then? Why can't we see their space ship?'

Nathen switched the microphone on in a gesture that showed the bitterness of his disappointment.

'We'll need a magnifying glass for that.'

THE COLD EQUATIONS

TOM GODWIN

HE WAS not alone.

There was nothing to indicate the fact but the white hand of the tiny gauge on the board before him. The control room was empty but for himself; there was no sound other than the murmur of the drives—but the white hand had moved. It had been on zero when the little ship was launched from the *Stardust*; now, an hour later, it had crept up. There was something in the supplies closet across the room, it was saying, some kind of body that radiated heat.

It could be but one kind of a body—a living, human body.

He leaned back in the pilot's chair and drew a deep, slow breath, considering what he would have to do. He was an EDS pilot, inured to the sight of death, long since accustomed to it and to viewing the dying of another man with an objective lack of emotion, and he had no choice in what he must do. There could be no alternative—but it required a few moments of conditioning for even an EDS pilot to prepare himself to walk across the room and coldly, deliberately, take the life of a man he had yet to meet.

He would, of course, do it. It was the law, stated very bluntly and definitely in grim Paragraph L, Section 8, of Interstellar Regulations: *Any stowaway discovered in an EDS shall be jettisoned immediately following discovery.*

It was the law, and there could be no appeal.

It was a law not of men's choosing but made imperative by the circumstances of the space frontier. Galactic expansion had followed the development of the hyperspace drive and as men scattered wide across the frontier there had come the problem of contact with the isolated first-colonies and exploration parties. The huge hyperspace cruisers were the product of the combined genius and effort of Earth and were long and expensive in the building. They were not available in such numbers that small colonies could possess them. The cruisers carried the colonists to their new worlds and made periodic visits, running on tight schedules, but they could not stop and turn aside to visit colonies scheduled to be visited at another time; such a delay would destroy their schedule and produce a confusion and uncertainty that would wreck the complex interdependence between old Earth and the new worlds of the frontier.

Some method of delivering supplies or assistance when an emergency occurred on a world not scheduled for a visit had been needed and the Emergency Dispatch Ships had been the answer. Small and collapsible, they occupied little room in the hold of the cruiser; made of light metal and plastics, they were driven by a small rocket drive that consumed relatively little fuel. Each cruiser carried four EDS's and when a call for aid was received the nearest cruiser would drop into normal space long enough to launch an EDS with the needed supplies or personnel, then vanish again as it continued on its course.

The cruisers, powered by nuclear converters, did not use the liquid rocket fuel but nuclear converters were far too large and complex to permit their installation in the EDS's. The cruisers were forced by necessity to carry a limited amount of the bulky rocket fuel and the fuel was rationed with care; the cruiser's computers determining the exact amount of fuel each EDS would require for its mission.

The computers considered the course co-ordinates, the mass of the EDS, the mass of pilot and cargo; they were very precise and accurate and omitted nothing from their calculations. They could not, however, foresee, and allow for, the added mass of a stowaway.

The *Stardust* had received the request from one of the exploration parties stationed on Woden; the six men of the party already being stricken with fever carried by the green *kala* midges and their own supply of serum destroyed by tornado that had torn through their camp. The *Stardust* had gone through the usual procedure; dropping into normal space to launch the EDS with the fever serum, then vanishing again in hyperspace. Now, an hour later, the gauge was saying there was something more than the small carton of serum in the supplies closet.

He let his eyes rest on the narrow white door of the closet. There, just inside, another man lived and breathed and was beginning to feel assured that discovery of his presence would now be too late for the pilot to alter the situation. It *was* too late—for the man behind the door it was far later than he thought and in a way he would find terrible to believe.

There could be no alternative. Additional fuel would be used during the hours of deceleration to compensate for the added mass of the stowaway; infinitesimal increments of fuel that would not be missed until the ship had almost reached its destination. Then, at some distance above the ground that might be as near as a thousand feet or as far as tens of thousands of feet, depending upon the mass of ship and cargo and the preceding period of deceleration, the unmissed increments of fuel would make their absence known; the EDS would expend its last drops of fuel with a sputter and go into whistling free fall. Ship and pilot and stowaway would merge together upon impact as a wreckage of metal and plastic, flesh and blood, driven deep into the soil. The stowaway had signed his own death warrant when he concealed himself on the ship; he could not be permitted to take seven others with him.

He looked again at the tell-tale white hand, then rose to his feet. What he must do would be unpleasant for both of them; the sooner it was over, the better. He stepped across the control room, to stand by the white door.

'Come out!' His command was harsh and abrupt above the murmur of the drive.

It seemed he could hear the whisper of a furtive movement inside the closet, then nothing. He visualized the stowaway cowering into one corner, suddenly worried by the possible consequences of his act and his self-assurance evaporating.

'I said *out*!'

He heard the stowaway move to obey and he waited with his eyes alert on the door and his hand near the blaster at his side.

The door opened and the stowaway stepped through it, smiling. 'All right—I give up. Now what?'

It was a girl.

He stared without speaking, his hand dropping away from the blaster and acceptance of what he saw coming like a heavy and unexpected physical blow. The stowaway was not a man—she was a girl in her teens, standing before him in little white gypsy sandals with the top of her brown, curly head hardly higher than his shoulder, with a faint, sweet scent of perfume coming from her and her smiling face tilted up so that her eyes could look unknowing and unafraid into his as she waited for his answer.

Now what? Had it been asked in the deep, defiant voice of a man he would have answered it with action, quick and efficient. He would have taken the stowaway's identification disc and ordered him into the air lock. Had the stowaway refused to obey, he would have used the blaster. It would not have taken long; within a minute the body would have been ejected into space—had the stowaway been a man.

He returned to the pilot's chair and motioned her to seat herself on the box-like bulk of the drive-control units that were set against the wall beside him. She obeyed, his silence making the smile fade into the meek and guilty expression of a pup that has been caught in mischief and knows it must be punished.

'You still haven't told me,' she said. 'I'm guilty, so what happens to me now? Do I pay a fine, or what?'

'What are you doing here?' he asked. 'Why did you stow away on this EDS?'

'I wanted to see my brother. He's with the government survey crew on Woden and I haven't seen him for ten years, not since he left Earth to go into government survey work.'

'What was your destination on the *Stardust*?'

'Mimir. I have a position waiting for me there. My brother has been sending money home all the time to us— my father and my mother and I—and he paid for a special course in linguistics I was taking. I graduated sooner than expected and I was offered this job on Mimir. I knew it would be almost a year before Gerry's job was done on Woden so he could come on to Mimir and that's why I hid in the closet, there. There was plenty of room for me and I was willing to pay the fine. There were only the two of us kids—Gerry and I—and I haven't seen him for so long, and I didn't want to wait another year when I could see him now, even though I knew I would be breaking some kind of a regulation when I did it.'

I knew I would be breaking some kind of a regulation—— In a way, she could not be blamed for her ignorance of the law; she was of Earth and had not realized that the laws of the space frontier must, of necessity, be as hard and relentless as the environment that gave them birth. Yet, to protect such as her from the results of their own ignorance of the frontier, there had been a sign over the door that led to the section of the *Stardust* that housed the EDS's, a sign that was plain for all to see and heed :

UNAUTHORIZED PERSONNEL
KEEP OUT!

'Does your brother know that you took a passage on the *Stardust* for Mimir?'

'Oh, yes. I sent him a spacegram telling him about my graduation and about going to Mimir on the *Stardust* a month before I left Earth. I already knew Mimir was where he would be stationed in a little over a year. He gets a promotion then, and he'll be based on Mimir and not have to stay out a year at a time on field trips, like he does now.'

There were two different survey groups on Woden, and he asked, 'What is his name?'

'Cross—Gerry Cross. He's in Group Two—that was the way his address read. Do you know him?'

Group One had requested the serum; Group Two was eight thousand miles away, across the Western Sea.

'No, I've never met him,' he said, then turned to the control board and cut the deceleration to a fraction of gravity; knowing as he did so that it could not avert the ultimate end, yet doing the only thing he could do to prolong that ultimate end. The sensation was like that of a ship suddenly dropping and the girl's involuntary movement of surprise half lifted her from her seat.

'We're going faster now, aren't we?' she asked. 'Why are we doing that?'

He told her the truth. 'To save fuel for a little while.'

'You mean we don't have very much?'

He delayed the answer he must give her so soon to ask: 'How did you manage to stow away?'

'I just sort of walked in when no one was looking my way,' she said. 'I was practising my Gelanese on the native girl who does the cleaning in the Ship's Supply Office when someone came in with an order for supplies for the survey crew on Woden. I slipped into the closet there after the ship was ready to go and just before you came in. It was an impulse of the moment to stow away, so I could get to see Gerry—and from the way you keep looking at me so grim, I'm not sure it was a very wise impulse.

'But I'll be a model criminal—or do I mean prisoner?' She smiled at him again. 'I intended to pay for my keep on top of paying the fine. I can cook and I can patch clothes for everyone and I know how to do all kinds of useful things, even a little bit about nursing.'

There was one more question to ask:

'Did you know what the supplies were that the survey crew ordered?'

'Why, no. Equipment they needed in their work, I supposed.'

Why couldn't she have been a man with some ulterior motive? A fugitive from justice, hoping to lose himself on a raw new world; an opportunist, seeking transportation to the new colonies where he might find golden fleece for the taking; a crackpot, with a mission——

Perhaps once in his lifetime an EDS pilot would find such a stowaway on his ship; warped men, mean and selfish men, brutal and dangerous men—but never, before, a smiling, blue-eyed girl who was willing to pay her fine and work for her keep that she might see her brother.

He turned to the board and turned the switch that would signal the *Stardust*. The call would be futile but he could not, until he had exhausted that one vain hope, seize her and thrust her into the air lock as he would an animal—or a man. The delay, in the meantime, would not be dangerous with the EDS decelerating at fractional gravity.

A voice spoke from the communicator. '*Stardust*. Identify yourself and proceed.'

'Barton, EDS 34G11. Emergency. Give me Commander Delhart.'

There was a faint confusion of noises as the request went through the proper channels. The girl was watching him, no longer smiling.

'Are you going to order them to come back after me?' she asked.

The communicator clicked and there was the sound of a distant voice saying, 'Commander, the EDS requests——'

'Are they coming back after me?' she asked again. 'Won't I get to see my brother, after all?'

'Barton?' The blunt, gruff voice of Commander Delhart came from the communicator. 'What's this about an emergency?'

'A stowaway,' he answered.

'A stowaway?' There was a slight surprise to the question. 'That's rather unusual—but why the "emergency" call? You discovered him in time so there should be no appreciable danger and I presume you've informed Ship's Records so his nearest relatives can be notified.'

'That's why I had to call you first. The stowaway is still aboard and the circumstances are so different——'

'Different?' the commander interrupted, impatience in his voice. 'How can they be different? You know you have a limited supply of fuel; you also know the law, as well as I do: "Any stowaway discovered in an EDS shall be jettisoned immediately following discovery." '

There was the sound of a sharply indrawn breath from the girl. *'What does he mean?'*

'The stowaway is a girl.'

'What?'

'She wanted to see her brother. She's only a kid and she didn't know what she was really doing.'

'I see.' All the curtness was gone from the commander's voice. 'So you called me in the hope I could do something?' Without waiting for an answer he went on. 'I'm sorry—I can do nothing. This cruiser must maintain its schedule; the life of not one person but the lives of many depend on it. I know how you feel but I'm powerless to help you

You'll have to go through with it. I'll have you connected
with Ship's Records.'

The communicator faded to a faint rustle of sound
and he turned to the girl. She was leaning forward
on the bench, almost rigid, her eyes fixed wide and
frightened.

'What did he mean, to go through with it? To jettison
me . . . to go through with it—what did he mean? Not
the way it sounded . . . he couldn't have. What did he
mean . . . what did he really mean?'

Her time was too short for the comfort of a lie to be
more than a cruelly fleeting delusion.

'He meant it the way it sounded.'

'*No!*' She recoiled from him as though he had struck her,
one hand half upraised as though to fend him off and stark
unwillingness to believe in her eyes.

'It will have to be.'

'No! You're joking—you're insane! You can't mean it!'

'I'm sorry.' He spoke slowly to her, gently. 'I should
have told you before—I should have, but I had to do what
I could first; I had to call the *Stardust*. You heard what the
commander said.'

'But you can't—if you make me leave the ship, I'll *die*.'

'I know.'

She searched his face and the unwillingness to believe
left her eyes, giving way slowly to a look of dazed terror.

'You—know?' She spoke the words far apart, numb and
wonderingly.

'I know. It has to be like that.'

'You mean it—you really mean it.' She sagged back
against the wall, small and limp like a little rag doll and all
the protesting and disbelief gone. 'You're going to do it—
you're going to make me die?'

'I'm sorry,' he said again. 'You'll never know how sorry
I am. It has to be that way and no human in the universe
can change it.'

'You're going to make me die and I didn't do anything to die for—I didn't *do* anything——'

He sighed, deep and weary. 'I know you didn't, child. I know you didn't——'

'EDS.' The communicator rapped brisk and metallic. 'This is Ship's Records. Give us all information on subject's identification disc.'

He got out of his chair to stand over her. She clutched the edge of the seat, her upturned face white under the brown hair and the lipstick standing out like a blood-red cupid's bow.

'*Now?*'

'I want your identification disc,' he said.

She released the edge of the seat and fumbled at the chain that suspended the plastic disc from her neck with fingers that were trembling and awkward. He reached down and unfastened the clasp for her, then returned with the disc to his chair.

'Here's your data, Records: Identification Number T837——'

'One moment,' Records interrupted. 'This is to be filed on the grey card, of course?'

'Yes.'

'And the time of the execution?'

'I'll tell you later.'

'Later? This is highly irregular; the time of the subject's death is required before——'

He kept the thickness out of his voice with an effort. 'Then we'll do it in a highly irregular manner—you'll hear the disc read first. The subject is a girl and she's listening to everything that's said. Are you capable of understanding that?'

There was a brief, almost shocked, silence, then Records said meekly : 'Sorry. Go ahead.'

He began to read the disc, reading it slowly to delay the inevitable for as long as possible, trying to help her by giving her what little time he could to recover from her first terror and let it resolve into the calm of acceptance and resignation.

'Number T8374 dash Y54. Name: Marilyn Lee Cross. Sex: Female. Born: July 7, 2160. *She was only eighteen.* Height: 5 3. Weight: 110. *Such a slight weight, yet enough to add fatally to the mass of the shell-thin bubble that was an EDS.* Hair: Brown. Eyes: Blue. Complexion: Light. Blood Type: O. *Irrelevant data.* Destination: Port City Mimir. *Invalid data——*'

He finished and said, 'I'll call you later,' then turned once again to the girl. She was huddled back against the wall, watching him with a look of numb and wondering fascination.

'They're waiting for you to kill me, aren't they? They want me dead, don't they? You and everybody on the cruiser wants me dead, don't you?' Then the numbness broke and her voice was that of a frightened and bewildered child. 'Everybody wants me dead and I didn't *do* anything. I didn't hurt anyone—I only wanted to see my brother.'

'It's not the way you think—it isn't that way, at all,' he said. 'Nobody wants it this way; nobody would ever let it be this way if it was humanly possible to change it.'

'Then why is it? I don't understand. Why is it?'

'This ship is carrying *kala* fever serum to Group One on Woden. Their own supply was destroyed by a tornado. Group Two—the crew your brother is in—is eight thousand miles away across the Western Sea and their helicopters can't cross it to help Group One. The fever is invariably fatal unless the serum can be had in time, and the six men in Group One will die unless this ship reaches them on schedule. These little ships are always given barely enough fuel to reach their destination and if you stay aboard your added weight will cause it to use up all its fuel before it reaches the ground. It will crash, then, and you and I will die and so will the six men waiting for the fever serum.'

It was a full minute before she spoke, and as she considered his words the expression of numbness left her eyes.

'Is that it?' she asked at last. 'Just that the ship doesn't have enough fuel?'

'Yes.'

'I can go alone or I can take seven others with me—is that the way it is?'

'That's the way it is.'

'And nobody wants me to have to die?'

'Nobody.'

'Then maybe—— Are you sure nothing can be done about it? Wouldn't people help me if they could?'

'Everyone would like to help you but there is nothing anyone can do. I did the only thing I could when I called the *Stardust*.'

'And it won't come back—but there might be other cruisers, mightn't there? Isn't there any hope at all that there might be someone, somewhere, who could do something to help me?'

She was leaning forward a little in her eagerness as she waited for his answer.

'No.'

The word was like the drop of a cold stone and she again leaned back against the wall, the hope and eagerness leaving her face. 'You're sure—you *know* you're sure?'

'I'm sure. There are no other cruisers within forty light-years; there is nothing and no one to change things.'

She dropped her gaze to her lap and began twisting a pleat of her skirt between her fingers, saying no more as her mind began to adapt itself to the grim knowledge.

It was better so; with the going of all hope would go the fear; with the going of all hope would come resignation. She needed time and she could have so little of it. How much?

The EDS's were not equipped with hull-cooling units; their speed had to be reduced to a moderate level before entering the atmosphere. They were decelerating at ·10 gravity; approaching their destination at a far higher speed than the computers had calculated on. The *Stardust* had

D

been quite near Woden when she launched the EDS; their present velocity was putting them nearer by the second. There would be a critical point, soon to be reached, when he would have to resume deceleration. When he did so the girl's weight would be multiplied by the gravities of deceleration, would become, suddenly, a factor of paramount importance; the factor the computers had been ignorant of when they determined the amount of fuel the EDS should have. She would have to go when deceleration began; it could be no other way. When would that be—how long could he let her stay?

'How long can I stay?'

He winced involuntarily from the words that were so like an echo of his own thoughts. How long? He didn't know; he would have to ask the ship's computers. Each EDS was given a meagre supply of fuel to compensate for unfavourable conditions within the atmosphere and relatively little fuel was being consumed for the time being. The memory banks of the computers would still contain all the data pertaining to the course set for the EDS; such data would not be erased until the EDS reached its destination. He had only to give the computers the new data; the girl's weight and the exact time at which he had reduced the deceleration to ·10.

'Barton.' Commander Delhart's voice came abruptly from the communicator, as he opened his mouth to call the *Stardust*. 'A check with Records shows me you haven't completed your report. Did you reduce the deceleration?'

So the commander knew what he was trying to do.

'I'm decelerating at point ten,' he answered. 'I cut the deceleration at seventeen fifty and the weight is a hundred and ten. I would like to stay at point ten as long as the computers say I can. Will you give them the question?'

It was contrary to regulations for an EDS pilot to make any changes in the course or degree of deceleration the computers had set for him but the commander made no mention of the violation, neither did he ask the reason for it. It was not necessary for him to ask; he had not become commander of an interstellar cruiser without both intelligence and an understanding of human nature. He said only : 'I'll have that given the computers.'

The communicator fell silent and he and the girl waited, neither of them speaking. They would not have to wait long; the computers would give the answer within moments of the asking. The new factors would be fed into the steel maw of the first bank and the electrical impulses would go through the complex circuits. Here and there a relay might click, a tiny cog turn over, but it would be essentially the electrical impulses that found the answer; formless, mindless, invisible, determining with utter precision how long the pale girl beside him might live. Then five little segments of metal in the second bank would trip in rapid succession against an inked ribbon and a second steel maw would spit out the slip of paper that bore the answer.

The chronometer on the instrument board read 18.10 when the commander spoke again.

'You will resume deceleration at nineteen ten.'

She looked towards the chronometer, then quickly away from it. 'Is that when . . . when I go?' she asked. He nodded and she dropped her eyes to her lap again.

'I'll have the course corrections given you,' the commander said. 'Ordinarily I would never permit anything like this but I understand your position. There is nothing I can do, other than what I've just done, and you will not deviate from these new instructions. You will complete your report at nineteen ten. Now—here are the course corrections.'

The voice of some unknown technician read them to him and he wrote them down on a pad clipped to the edge of the control board. There would, he saw, be periods of deceleration when he neared the atmosphere when the deceleration would be five gravities—and at five gravities, one hundred and ten pounds would become five hundred and fifty pounds.

The technician finished and he terminated the contact

with a brief acknowledgment. Then, hesitating a moment, he reached out and shut off the communicator. It was 18.13 and he would have nothing to report until 19.10. In the meantime, it somehow seemed indecent to permit others to hear what she might say in her last hour.

He began to check the instrument readings, going over them with unnecessary slowness. She would have to accept the circumstances and there was nothing he could do to help her into acceptance; words of sympathy would only delay it.

It was 18.20 when she stirred from her motionlessness and spoke.

'So that's the way it has to be with me?'

He swung around to face her. 'You understand now, don't you? No one would ever let it be like this if it could be changed.'

'I understand,' she said. Some of the colour had returned to her face and the lipstick no longer stood out so vividly red. 'There isn't enough fuel for me to stay; when I hid on this ship I got into something I didn't know anything about and now I have to pay for it.'

She had violated a man-made law that said KEEP OUT but the penalty was not of men's making or desire and it was a penalty men could not revoke. A physical law had decreed: *h amount of fuel will power an EDS with a mass of m safely to its destination;* and a second physical law decreed: *h amount of fuel will not power an EDS with a mass of m plus x safely to its destination.*

EDS's obeyed only physical laws and no amount of human sympathy for her could alter the second law.

'But I'm afraid. I don't want to die—not now. I want to live and nobody is doing anything to help me; everybody is letting me go ahead and acting just like nothing was going to happen to me. I'm going to die and nobody *cares.*'

'We all do,' he said. 'I do and the commander does and the clerk in Ship's Records; we all care and each of us did what little he could to help you. It wasn't enough—it was almost nothing—but it was all we could do.'

'Not enough fuel—I can understand that,' she said, as though she had not heard his own words. 'But to have to die for it. *Me*, alone——'

How hard it must be for her to accept the fact. She had never known danger of death; had never known the environments where the lives of men could be as fragile and as fleeting as sea foam tossed against a rocky shore. She belonged on gentle Earth, in that secure and peaceful society where she could be young and gay and laughing with others of her kind; where life was precious and well-guarded and there was always the assurance that tomorrow would come. She belonged to that world of soft winds and warm suns, music and moonlight and gracious manners and not on the hard, bleak frontier.

'How did it happen to me, so terribly quickly? An hour ago I was on the *Stardust*, going to Mimir. Now the *Stardust* is going on without me and I'm going to die and I'll never see Gerry and Mama and Daddy again—I'll never see anything again.'

He hesitated, wondering how he could explain it to her so that she would really understand and not feel she had, somehow, been the victim of a reasonlessly cruel injustice. She did not know what the frontier was like; she thought in terms of safe-and-secure Earth. Pretty girls were not jettisoned on Earth; there was a law against it. On Earth her plight would have filled the newscasts and a fast black Patrol ship would have been racing to her rescue. Everyone, everywhere, would have known of Marilyn Lee Cross and no effort would have been spared to save her life. But this was not Earth and there were no Patrol ships; only the *Stardust*, leaving them behind at many times the speed of light. There was no one to help her, there would be no Marilyn Lee Cross smiling from the newscasts tomorrow. Marilyn Lee Cross would be but a poignant memory for an EDS pilot and a name on a grey card in Ship's Records.

'It's different here; it's not like back on Earth,' he said. 'It isn't that no one cares; it's that no one can do anything to help. The frontier is big and here along its rim the colonies and exploration parties are scattered so thin and far between. On Woden, for example, there are only sixteen men—sixteen men on an entire world. The exploration parties, the survey crews, the little first-colonies—they're all fighting alien environments, trying to make a way for those who will follow after. The environments fight back and those who go first usually make mistakes only once. There is no margin of safety along the rim of the frontier; there can't be until the way is made for the others who will come later, until the new worlds are tamed and settled. Until then men will have to pay the penalty for making mistakes with no one to help them because there is no one *to* help them.'

'I was going to Mimir,' she said. 'I didn't know about the frontier; I was only going to Mimir and *it's* safe.'

'Mimir is safe but you left the cruiser that was taking you there.'

She was silent for a little while. 'It was all so wonderful at first; there was plenty of room for me on this ship and I would be seeing Gerry so soon . . . I didn't know about the fuel, didn't know what would happen to me——'

Her words trailed away and he turned his attention to the view-screen, not wanting to stare at her as she fought her way through the black horror of fear towards the calm grey of acceptance.

Woden was a ball, enshrouded in the blue haze of atmosphere, swimming in space against the background of star-sprinkled dead blackness. The great mass of Manning's Continent sprawled like a gigantic hourglass in the Eastern Sea with the western half of the Eastern Continent still visible. There was a thin line of shadow along the right-hand edge of the globe and the Eastern Continent was disappearing into it as the planet turned on its axis. An hour before the entire continent had been in view, now a thousand miles of it had gone into the thin edge of shadow and around to the night that lay on the other side of the world. The dark blue spot that was Lotus Lake was approaching the shadow. It was somewhere near the southern edge of the lake that Group Two had their camp. It would be night there, soon, and quick behind the coming of night the rotation of Woden on its axis would put Group Two beyond the reach of the ship's radio.

He would have to tell her before it was too late for her to talk to her brother. In a way, it would be better for both of them should they not do so but it was not for him to decide. To each of them the last words would be something to hold and cherish, something that would cut like the blade of a knife yet would be infinitely precious to remember, she for her own brief moments to live and he for the rest of his life.

He held down the button that would flash the grid lines on the viewscreen and used the known diameter of the planet to estimate the distance the southern tip of Lake Lotus had yet to go until it passed beyond radio range. It was approximately five hundred miles. Five hundred miles; thirty minutes—and the chronometer read 18.30 Allowing for error in estimating, it could not be later than 19.05 that the turning of Woden would cut off her brother's voice.

The first border of the Western Continent was already in sight along the left side of the world. Four thousand miles across it lay the shore of the Western Sea and the Camp of Group One. It had been in the Western Sea that the tornado had originated, to strike with such fury at the camp and destroy half their prefabricated buildings, including the one that housed the medical supplies. Two days before the tornado had not existed; it had been no more than great gentle masses of air out over the calm Western Sea. Group One had gone about their routine survey work, unaware of the meeting of the air masses out at sea, unaware of the

force the union was spawning. It had struck their camp
without warning; a thundering, roaring destruction that
sought to annihilate all that lay before it. It had passed on,
leaving the wreckage in its wake. It had destroyed the
labour of months and had doomed six men to die and then,
as though its task was accomplished, it once more began
to resolve into gentle masses of air. But for all its deadli-
ness, it had destroyed with neither malice nor intent. It
had been a blind and mindless force, obeying the laws of
nature, and it would have followed the same course with
the same fury had man never existed.

Existence required Order and there was order; the laws
of nature, irrevocable and immutable. Men could learn to
use them but men could not change them. The circumfer-
ence of a circle was always pi times the diameter and no
science of Man would ever make it otherwise. The combination of chemical A with chemical B under condition C
invariably produced reaction D. The law of gravitation was
a rigid equation and it made no distinction between the
fall of a leaf and the ponderous circling of a binary star
system. The nuclear conversion process powered the
cruisers that carried men to the stars; the same process in
the form of a nova would destroy a world with equal
efficiency. The laws *were*, and the universe moved in obe-
dience to them. Along the frontier were arrayed all the
forces of nature and sometimes they destroyed those who
were fighting their way outwards from Earth. The men of
the frontier had long ago learned the bitter futility of cursing the forces that would destroy them for the forces were
blind and deaf; the futility of looking to the heavens for
mercy, for the stars of the galaxy swung in their long, long
sweep of two hundred million years, as inexorably controlled as they by the laws that knew neither hatred nor
compassion.

The men of the frontier knew—but how was a girl from
Earth to fully understand? *H amount of fuel will not power
an EDS with a mass of m plus x safely to its destination.*

To himself and her brother and parents she was a sweet-faced girl in her teens; to the laws of nature she was x, the unwanted factor in a cold equation.

She stirred again on the seat. 'Could I write a letter? I want to write to Mama and Daddy and I'd like to talk to Gerry. Could you let me talk to him over your radio there?'

'I'll try to get him,' he said.

He switched on the normal-space transmitter and pressed the signal button. Someone answered the button almost immediately.

'Hello. How's it going with you fellows now—is the EDS on its way?'

'This isn't Group One; this is the EDS,' he said. 'Is Gerry Cross there?'

'Gerry? He and two others went out in the helicopter this morning and aren't back yet. It's almost sundown, though, and he ought to be back right away—in less than an hour at the most.'

'Can you connect me through the radio in his 'copter?'

'Huh-uh. It's been out of commission for two months—some printed circuits went haywire and we can't get any more until the next cruiser stops by. Is it something important—bad news for him, or something?'

'Yes—it's very important. When he comes in get him to the transmitter as soon as you possibly can.'

'I'll do that; I'll have one of the boys waiting at the field with a truck. Is there anything else I can do?'

'No, I guess that's all. Get him there as soon as you can and sign me.'

He turned the volume to an inaudible minimum, an act that would not affect the functioning of the signal buzzer, and unclipped the pad of paper from the control board. He tore off the sheet containing his flight instructions and handed the pad to her, together with pencil.

'I'd better write to Gerry, too,' she said as she took them. 'He might not get back to camp in time.'

She began to write, her fingers still clumsy and uncertain in the way they handled the pencil and the top of it trembling a little as she poised it between words. He turned back to the viewscreen, to stare at it without seeing it.

She was a lonely little child, trying to say her last good-bye, and she would lay out her heart to them. She would tell them how much she loved them and she would tell them to not feel badly about it, that it was only something that must eventually happen to everyone and she was not afraid. The last would be a lie and it would be there to read between the sprawling, uneven lines; a valiant little lie that would make the hurt all the greater for them.

Her brother was of the frontier and he would understand. He would not hate the EDS pilot for doing nothing to prevent her going; he would know there had been nothing the pilot could do. He would understand, though the understanding would not soften the shock and pain when he learned his sister was gone. But the others, her father and mother—they would not understand. They were of Earth and they would think in the manner of those who had never lived where the safety margin of life was a thin, thin line—and sometimes not at all. What would they think of the faceless, unknown pilot who had sent her to her death?

They would hate him with cold and terrible intensity, but it really didn't matter. He would never see them, never know them. He would have only the memories to remind him; only the nights to fear, when a blue-eyed girl in gypsy sandals would come in his dreams to die again——

He scowled at the viewscreen and tried to force his thoughts into less emotional channels. There was nothing he could do to help her. She had unknowingly subjected herself to the penalty of a law that recognized neither innocence nor youth nor beauty, that was incapable of sympathy or leniency. Regret was illogical—and yet, could knowing it to be illogical ever keep it away?

She stopped occasionally, as though trying to find the right words to tell them what she wanted them to know, then the pencil would resume its whispering to the paper. It was 18.37 when she folded the letter in a square and wrote a name on it. She began writing another, twice looking up at the chronometer as though she feared the black hand might reach its rendezvous before she had finished. It was 18.45 when she folded it as she had done the first letter and wrote a name and address on it.

She held the letters out to him. 'Will you take care of these and see that they're enveloped and mailed?'

'Of course.' He took them from her hand and placed them in a pocket of his grey uniform shirt.

'These can't be sent off until the next cruiser stops by and the *Stardust* will have long since told them about me, won't it?' she asked. He nodded and she went on. 'That makes the letters not important in one way but in another way they're very important—to me, and to them.'

'I know, I understand, and I'll take care of them.'

She glanced at the chronometer, then back at him. 'It seems to move faster all the time, doesn't it?'

He said nothing, unable to think of anything to say, and she asked, 'Do you think Gerry will come back to camp in time?'

'I think so. They said he should be in right away.'

She began to roll the pencil back and forth between her palms. 'I hope he does. I feel sick and scared and I want to hear his voice again and maybe I won't feel so alone. I'm a coward and I can't help it.'

'No,' he said, 'you're not a coward. You're afraid, but you're not a coward.'

'Is there a difference?'

He nodded. 'A lot of difference.'

'I feel so alone. I never did feel like this before; like I was all by myself and there was nobody to care what happened to me. Always, before, there was Mama and Daddy there and my friends around me. I had lots of friends, and

they had a going-away party for me the night before I
left.'

Friends and music and laughter for her to remember—
and on the viewscreen Lotus Lake was going into the
shadow.

'Is it the same with Gerry?' she asked. 'I mean, if he
should make a mistake, would he have to die for it, all
alone and with no one to help him?'

'It's the same with all along the frontier; it will always
be like that so long as there is a frontier.'

'Gerry didn't tell us. He said the pay was good and he
sent money home all the time because Daddy's little shop
just brought in a bare living, but he didn't tell us it was
like this.'

'He didn't tell you his work was dangerous?'

'Well—yes. He mentioned that, but we didn't understand. I always thought danger along the frontier was
something that was a lot of fun; an exciting adventure, like
the three-D shows.' A wan smile touched her face for a
moment. 'Only it's not, is it? It's not the same at all,
because when it's real you can't go home after the show
is over.'

'No,' he said. 'No, you can't.'

Her glance flicked from the chronometer to the door of
the air lock, then down to the pad and pencil she still held.
She shifted her position slightly to lay them on the bench
beside her, moving one foot out a little. For the first time
he saw that she was not wearing Vegan gypsy sandals but
only cheap imitations; the expensive Vegan leather was
some kind of grained plastic, the silver buckle was gilded
iron, the jewels were coloured glass. *Daddy's little shop
just brought in a bare living*—— She must have left college
in her second year, to take the course in linguistics that
would enable her to make her own way and help her
brother provide for her parents, earning what she could by
part-time work after classes were over. Her personal pos-
sessions on the *Stardust* would be taken back to her parents

—they would neither be of much value nor occupy much storage space for the return voyage.

'Isn't it——' She stopped, and he looked at her questioningly. 'Isn't it cold in here?' she asked, almost apologetically. 'Doesn't it seem cold to you?'

'Why, yes,' he said. He saw by the main temperature gauge that the room was at precisely normal temperature. 'Yes, it's colder than it should be.'

'I wish Gerry would get back before it's too late. Do you really think he will, and you didn't say so just to make me feel better?'

'I think he will— they said he would be in pretty soon.' On the viewscreen Lotus Lake had gone into the shadow but for the thin blue line on its western edge, and it was apparent he had overestimated the time she would have in which to talk to her brother. Reluctantly, he said to her, 'His camp will be out of radio range in a few minutes; he's on that part of Woden that's in the shadow'—he indicated the viewscreen—'and the turning of Woden will put him beyond contact. There may not be much time left when he comes in—not much time to talk to him before he fades out. I wish I could do something about it—I would call him right now if I could.'

'Not even as much time as I will have to stay?'

'I'm afraid not.'

'Then——' She straightened and looked towards the air lock with pale resolution. 'Then I'll go when Gerry passes beyond range, I won't wait any longer after that—I won't have anything to wait for.'

Again there was nothing he could say.

'Maybe I shouldn't wait at all. Maybe I'm selfish—maybe it would be better for Gerry if you just told him about it afterwards.'

There was an unconscious pleading for denial in the way she spoke and he said, 'He wouldn't want you to do that, not to wait for him.'

'It's already coming dark where he is, isn't it? There will be all the long night before him, and Mama and Daddy don't know yet that I won't ever be coming back like I promised them I would. I've caused everyone I love to be hurt, haven't I? I didn't want to—I didn't intend to.'

'It wasn't your fault,' he said. 'It wasn't your fault at all. They'll know that. They'll understand.'

'At first I was so afraid to die that I was a coward and thought only of myself. Now, I see how selfish I was. The terrible thing about dying like this is not that I'll be gone but that I'll never see them again; never be able to tell them that I didn't take them for granted; never be able to tell them I knew of the sacrifices they made to keep my life happier, that I knew all the things they did for me and that I loved them so much more than I ever told them. I've never told them any of those things. You don't tell them such things when you're young and your life is all before you—you're afraid of sounding sentimental and silly.

'But it's so different when you have to die—you wish you had told them while you could and you wish you could tell them you're sorry for all the little mean things you ever did or said to them. You wish you could tell them that you didn't really mean to ever hurt their feelings and for them only to remember that you always loved them far more than you ever let them know.'

'You don't have to tell them that,' he said. 'They will know—they've always known it.'

'Are you sure?' she asked. 'How can you be sure? My people are strangers to you.'

'Wherever you go, human nature and human hearts are the same.'

'And they will know what I want them to know—that I love them?'

'They've always known it, in a way far better than you could ever put in words for them.'

'I keep remembering the things they did for me, and it's

the little things they did that seem to be the most important to me, now. Like Gerry—he sent me a bracelet of fire-rubies on my sixteenth birthday. It was beautiful—it must have cost him a month's pay. Yet, I remember him more for what he did the night my kitten got run over in the street. I was only six years old and he held me in his arms and wiped away my tears and told me not to cry, that Flossy was gone for just a little while, for just long enough to get herself a new fur coat and she would be on the foot of my bed the very next morning. I believed him and quit crying and went to sleep dreaming about my kitten coming back. When I woke up the next morning, there was Flossy on the foot of my bed in a brand-new white fur coat, just like he had said she would be.

'It wasn't until a long time later that Mama told me Gerry had got the pet-shop owner out of bed at four in the morning and, when the man got mad about it, Gerry told him he was either going to go down and sell him the white kitten right then or he'd break his neck.'

'It's always the little things you remember people by; all the little things they did because they wanted to do them for you. You've done the same for Gerry and your father and mother; all kinds of things that you've forgotten about but they will never forget.'

'I hope I have. I would like for them to remember me like that.'

'They will.'

'I wish——' She swallowed. 'The way I'll die—I wish they wouldn't ever think of that. I've read how people look who have died in space—their insides all ruptured and exploded and their lungs out between their teeth and then, a few seconds later, they're all dry and shapeless and horribly ugly. I don't want them to ever think of me as something dead and horrible, like that.'

'You're their own, their child and their sister. They could never think of you other than the way you want them to; the way you looked the last time they saw you.'

'I'm still afraid,' she said. 'I can't help it, but I don't want Gerry to know it. If he gets back in time, I'm going to act like I'm not afraid at all and——'

The signal buzzer interrupted her, quick and imperative.

'Gerry!' She came to her feet. 'It's Gerry, now!'

He spun the volume control knob and asked: 'Gerry Cross?'

'Yes,' her brother answered, an undertone of tenseness to his reply. 'The bad news—what is it?'

She answered for him, standing close behind him and leaning down a little towards the communicator, her hand resting small and cold on his shoulder.

'Hello, Gerry.' There was only a faint quiver to betray the careful casualness of her voice. 'I wanted to see you——'

'Marilyn!' There was sudden and terrible apprehension in the way he spoke to her. 'What are you doing on that EDS?'

'I wanted to see you,' she said again. 'I wanted to see you, so I hid on this ship——'

'You *hid* on it?'

'I'm a stowaway . . . I didn't know what it would mean——'

'*Marilyn!*' It was the cry of a man who calls hopeless and desperate to someone already and forever gone from him. 'What have you done?'

'I . . . it's not——' Then her own composure broke and the cold little hand gripped his shoulder convulsively. 'Don't, Gerry—I only wanted to see you; I didn't intend to hurt you. Please, Gerry, don't feel like that——'

Something warm and wet splashed on his wrist and he slid out of the chair, to help her into it and swing the microphone down to her level.

'Don't feel like that—— Don't let me go knowing you feel like that——'

The sob she tried to hold back choked in her throat and her brother spoke to her. 'Don't cry, Marilyn.' His voice was suddenly deep and infinitely gentle, with all the pain held out of it. 'Don't cry, Sis—you mustn't do that. It's all right, Honey—everything is all right.'

'I——' Her lower lip quivered and she bit into it. 'I didn't want you to feel that way—I just wanted us to say good-bye because I have to go in a minute.'

'Sure—sure. That's the way it will be, Sis. I didn't mean to sound the way I did.' Then his voice changed to a tone of quick and urgent demand. 'EDS—have you called the *Stardust*? Did you check with the computers?'

'I called the *Stardust* almost an hour ago. It can't turn back, there are no other cruisers within forty light-years, and there isn't enough fuel.'

'Are you sure that the computers had the correct data—sure of everything?'

'Yes—do you think I could ever let it happen if I wasn't sure? I did everything I could do. If there was anything at all I could do now, I would do it?'

'He tried to help me, Gerry.' Her lower lip was no longer trembling and the short sleeves of her blouse were wet where she had dried her tears. 'No one can help me and I'm not going to cry any more and everything will be all right with you and Daddy and Mama, won't it?'

'Sure—sure it will. We'll make out fine.'

Her brother's words were beginning to come in more faintly and he turned the volume control to maximum. 'He's going out of range,' he said to her. 'He'll be gone within another minute.'

'You're fading out, Gerry,' she said. 'You're going out of range. I wanted to tell you—but I can't, now. We must say good-bye so soon—but maybe I'll see you again. Maybe I'll come to you in your dreams with my hair in braids and crying because the kitten in my arms is dead; maybe I'll be the touch of a breeze that whispers to you as it goes by; maybe I'll be one of those gold-winged larks you told me about, singing my silly head off to you; maybe, at times, I'll be nothing you can see but you will know I'm there

E

beside you. Think of me like that, Gerry; always like that and not—the other way.'

Dimmed to a whisper by the turning of Woden, the answer came back:

'Always like that, Marilyn—always like that and never any other way.'

'Our time is up, Gerry—I have to go, now. Good——'
Her voice broke in mid-word and her mouth tried to twist into crying. She pressed her hand hard against it and when she spoke again the words came clear and true:

'Good-bye, Gerry.'

Faint and ineffably poignant and tender, the last words came from the cold metal of the communicator.

'Good-bye, little sister——'

She sat motionless in the hush that followed, as though listening to the shadow-echoes of the words as they died away, then she turned away from the communicator towards the air lock, and he pulled down the black lever beside him. The inner door of the air lock slid swiftly open, to reveal the bare little cell that was waiting for her, and she walked to it.

She walked with her head up and the brown curls brushing her shoulders, with the white sandals stepping as sure and steady as the fractional gravity would permit and the gilded buckles twinkling with little lights of blue and red and crystal. He let her walk alone and made no move to help her, knowing she would not want it that way. She stepped into the air lock and turned to face him, only the pulse in her throat to betray the wild beating of her heart.

'I'm ready,' she said.

He pushed the lever up and the door slid its quick barrier between them, inclosing her in black and utter darkness for her last moments of life. It clicked as it locked in place and he jerked down the red lever. There was a slight waver to the ship as the air gushed from the lock, a vibration to the wall as though something had bumped the outer door in passing, then there was nothing and the ship was dropping true and steady again. He shoved the red lever back to close the door on the empty air lock and turned away, to walk to the pilot's chair with the slow steps of a man old and weary.

Back in the pilot's chair he pressed the signal button of the normal-space transmitter. There was no response; he had expected none. Her brother would have to wait through the night until the turning of Woden permitted contact through Group One.

It was not yet time to resume deceleration and he waited while the ship dropped endlessly downwards with him and the drives purred softly. He saw that the white hand of the supplies closet temperature was on zero. A cold equation had been balanced and he was alone on the ship. Something shapeless and ugly was hurrying ahead of him, going to Woden where its brother was waiting through the night, but the empty ship still lived for a little while with the presence of the girl who had not known about the forces that killed with neither hatred nor malice. It seemed, almost, that she still sat small and bewildered and frightened on the metal box beside him, her words echoing hauntingly clear in the void she had left behind her:

I didn't do anything to die for—I didn't do anything——

Time and the Fourth Dimension

A SOUND OF THUNDER

RAY BRADBURY

THE SIGN on the wall seemed to quaver under a film of sliding warm water. Eckels felt his eyelids blink over his stare, and the sign burned in this momentary darkness:

> TIME SAFARI, INC.
> SAFARIS TO ANY YEAR IN THE PAST.
> YOU NAME THE ANIMAL.
> WE TAKE YOU THERE.
> YOU SHOOT IT.

A warm phlegm gathered in Eckel's throat; he swallowed and pushed it down. The muscles around his mouth formed a smile as he put his hand slowly out upon the air, and in that hand waved a cheque for ten thousand dollars to the man behind the desk.

'Does this safari guarantee I come back alive?'

'We guarantee nothing,' said the official, 'except the dinosaurs.' He turned. 'This is Mr. Travis, your Safari Guide in the Past. He'll tell you what and where to shoot. If he says no shooting, no shooting. If you disobey instructions, there's a stiff penalty of another ten thousand dollars, plus possible government action, on your return.'

Eckels glanced across the vast office at a mass and tangle, a snaking and humming of wires and steel boxes, at an aurora that flickered now orange, now silver, now blue. There was a sound like a gigantic bonfire burning all of

Time, all the years and all the parchment calendars, all the hours piled high and set aflame.

A touch of the hand and this burning would, on the instant, beautifully reverse itself. Eckels remembered the wording in the advertisements to the letter. Out of chars and ashes, out of dust and coals, like golden salamanders, the old years, the green years, might leap; roses sweeten the air, white hair turn Irish-black, wrinkles vanish; all, everything fly back to seed, flee death, rush down to their beginnings, suns rise in western skies and set in glorious easts, moons eat themselves opposite to the custom, all and everything cupping one in another like Chinese boxes, rabbits into hats, all and everything returning to the fresh death, the seed death, the green death, to the time before the beginning. A touch of a hand might do it, the merest touch of a hand.

'Lord, Lord,' Eckels breathed, the light of the Machine on his thin face. 'A real Time Machine.' He shook his head. 'Makes you think. If the election had gone badly yesterday, I might be here now running away from the results. Thank God Keith won. He'll make a fine President of the United States.'

'Yes,' said the man behind the desk. 'We're lucky. If Deutscher had gotten in, we'd have the worst kind of dictatorship. There's an anti-everything man for you, a militarist, anti-Christ, anti-human, anti-intellectual. People called us up, you know, joking but not joking. Said if Deutscher became President they wanted to go live in 1492. Of course it's not our business to conduct Escapes, but to form Safaris. Anyway, Keith's President now. All you got to worry about is——'

'Shooting my dinosaur,' Eckels finished it for him.

'A *Tyrannosaurus rex*. The Thunder Lizard, the damnedest monster in history. Sign this please. Anything happens to you, we're not responsible. Those dinosaurs are hungry.'

Eckels flushed angrily. 'Trying to scare me!'

'Frankly, yes. We don't want anyone going who'll panic at the first shot. Six Safari leaders were killed last year, and a dozen hunters. We're here to give you the greatest thrill a *real* hunter ever asked for. Travelling you back sixty million years to bag the biggest game in all Time. Your personal cheque's still there. Tear it up.'

Mr. Eckels looked at the cheque for a long time. His fingers twitched.

'Good luck,' said the man behind the desk. 'Mr. Travis, he's all yours.'

They moved silently across the room, taking their guns with them, towards the Machine, towards the silver metal and the roaring light.

First a day and then a night and then a day and then a night, then it was day-night-day-night-day. A week, a month, a year, a decade! A.D. 2055. A.D. 2019. 1999! 1957! Gone! The Machine roared.

They put on their oxygen helmets and tested the intercoms.

Eckels swayed on the padded seat, his face pale, his jaw stiff. He felt the trembling in his arms and he looked down and found his hands tight on the new rifle. There were four other men in the Machine. Travis, the Safari Leader, his assistant, Lesperance, and two other hunters, Billings and Kramer. They sat looking at each other, and the years blazed around them.

'Can these guns get a dinosaur cold?' Eckels felt his mouth saying.

'If you hit them right,' said Travis on the helmet radio. 'Some dinosaurs have two brains, one in the head, another far down the spinal column. We stay away from those. That's stretching luck. Put your first two shots into the eyes, if you can, blind them, and go back into the brain.'

The Machine howled. Time was a film run backward. Suns fled and ten million moons fled after them. 'Good

God,' said Eckels. 'Every hunter that ever lived would envy us today. This makes Africa seem like Illinois.'

The Machine slowed; its scream fell to a murmur. The Machine stopped.

The sun stopped in the sky.

The fog that had enveloped the Machine blew away and they were in an old time, a very old time indeed, three hunters and two Safari Heads with their blue metal guns across their knees.

'Christ isn't born yet,' said Travis. 'Moses has not gone to the mountain to talk with God. The Pyramids are still in the earth, waiting to be cut out and put up. Remember that. Alexander, Cæsar, Napoleon, Hitler—none of them exists.'

The men nodded.

'That'—Mr. Travis pointed—'is the jungle of sixty million two thousand and fifty-five years before President Keith.'

He indicated a metal path that struck off into green wilderness, over steaming swamp, among giant ferns and palms.

'And that,' he said, 'is the Path, laid by Time Safari for your use. It floats six inches above the earth. Doesn't touch so much as one grass blade, flower, or tree. It's an anti-gravity metal. Its purpose is to keep you from touching this world of the past in any way. Stay on the Path. Don't go off it. I repeat. Don't go off. For any reason! If you fall off, there's a penalty. And don't shoot any animal we don't okay.'

'Why?' asked Eckels.

They sat in the ancient wilderness. Far birds' cries blew on a wind, and the smell of tar and an old salt sea, moist grasses, and flowers the colour of blood.

'We don't want to change the Future. We don't belong here in the Past. The government doesn't *like* us here. We have to pay big graft to keep our franchise. A Time Machine is damn finicky business. Not knowing it, we might kill an important animal, a small bird, a roach, a flower even, thus destroying an important link in a growing species.'

'That's not clear,' said Eckels.

'All right,' Travis continued, 'say we accidentally kill one mouse here. That means all the future families of this one particular mouse are destroyed, right?'

'Right.'

'And all the families of the families of the families of that one mouse! With a stamp of your foot, you annihilate first one, then a dozen, then a thousand, a million, a *billion* possible mice!'

'So they're dead,' said Eckels. 'So what?'

'So what?' Travis snorted quietly. 'Well, what about the foxes that'll need those mice to survive? For want of ten mice, a fox dies. For want of ten foxes, a lion starves. For want of a lion, all manner of insects, vultures, infinite billions of life forms are thrown into chaos and destruction. Eventually it all boils down to this: fifty-nine million years later, a cave man, one of a dozen on the *entire world*, goes hunting wild boar or sabre-tooth tiger for food. But you, friend, have *stepped* on all the tigers in that region. By stepping on *one* single mouse. So the cave man starves. And the cave man, please note, is not just *any* expendable man, no! He is an *entire future nation*. From his loins would have sprung ten sons. From *their* loins one hundred sons, and thus onward to a civilization. Destroy this one man, and you destroy a race, a people, an entire history of life. It is comparable to slaying some of Adam's grandchildren. The stomp of your foot, on one mouse, could start an earthquake, the effects of which could shake our earth and destinies down through Time, to their very foundations. With the death of that one cave man, a billion others yet unborn are throttled in the womb. Perhaps Rome never rises on its seven hills. Perhaps Europe is forever a dark forest, and only Asia waxes healthy and teeming. Step on a mouse and you crush the Pyramids. Step on a mouse and you leave your print, like a Grand Canyon, across Eternity. Queen Elizabeth might never be born, Washington might not cross the Delaware, there might never be a United States at all. So be careful. Stay on the Path. *Never* step off!'

'I see,' said Eckels. 'Then it wouldn't pay for us even to touch the *grass?*'

'Correct. Crushing certain plants could add up infinitesimally. A little error here would multiply in sixty million years, all out of proportion. Of course maybe our theory is wrong. Maybe Time *can't* be changed by us. Or maybe it can be changed only in little subtle ways. A dead mouse here makes an insect imbalance there, a population disproportion later, a bad harvest further on, a depression, mass starvation, and, finally, a change in *social* temperament in far-flung countries. Something much more subtle, like that. Perhaps only a soft breath, a whisper, a hair, pollen on the air, such a slight, slight change that unless you looked close you wouldn't see it. Who knows? Who really can say he knows? We don't know. We're guessing. But until we do know for certain whether our messing around in Time *can* make a big roar or a little rustle in history, we're being damned careful. This Machine, this Path, your clothing and bodies, were sterilized, as you know, before the journey. We wear these oxygen helmets so we can't introduce our bacteria into an ancient atmosphere.'

'How do we know which animals to shoot?'

'They're marked with red paint,' said Travis. 'Today, before our journey, we sent Lesperance here back with the Machine. He came to this particular era and followed certain animals.'

'Studying them?'

'Right,' said Lesperance. 'I track them through their entire existence, noting which of them lives longest. Very few. How many times they mate. Not often. Life's short. When I find one that's going to die when a tree falls on him, or one that drowns in a tar pit, I note the exact hour, minute, and second. I shoot a paint bomb. It leaves a red patch on his hide. We can't miss it. Then I correlate our arrival in the Past so that we meet the Monster not more than two minutes before he would have died anyway. This way, we kill only animals with no future, that are never going to mate again. You see how *careful* we are?'

'But if you came back this morning in Time,' said Eckels eagerly, 'you must've bumped into *us*, our Safari! How did it turn out? Was it successful? Did all of us get through —alive?'

Travis and Lesperance gave each other a look.

'That'd be a paradox,' said the latter. 'Time doesn't permit that sort of mess—a man meeting himself. When such occasions threaten, Time steps aside. Like an airplane hitting an air pocket. You felt the Machine jump just before we stopped? That was us passing ourselves on the way back to the Future. We saw nothing. There's no way of telling *if* this expedition was a success, *if we* got our monster, or whether all of us—meaning *you*, Mr. Eckels—got out alive.'

Eckels smiled palely.

'Cut that,' said Travis sharply. 'Everyone on his feet!'

They were ready to leave the Machine.

The jungle was high and the jungle was broad and the jungle was the entire world forever and forever. Sounds like music and sounds like flying tents filled the sky, and those were pterodactyls soaring with cavernous grey wings, gigantic bats out of delirium and a night fever. Eckels, balanced on the narrow Path, aimed his rifle playfully.

'Stop that!' said Travis. 'Don't even aim for fun, damn it! If your gun should go off——'

Eckels flushed. 'Where's our *Tyrannosaurus?*'

Lesperance checked his wrist watch. 'Up ahead. We'll bisect his trail in sixty seconds. Look for the red paint! Don't shoot till we give the word. Stay on the Path. *Stay on the Path!*'

They moved forward in the wind of morning.

'Strange,' murmured Eckels. 'Up ahead, sixty million

years, Election Day over. Keith made President. Everyone celebrating. And here we are, a million years lost, and they don't exist. The things we worried about for months, a lifetime, not even born or thought about yet.'

'Safety catches off, everyone!' ordered Travis. 'You, first shot, Eckels. Second, Billings. Third, Kramer.'

'I've hunted tiger, wild boar, buffalo, elephant, but this, oh, this, this is *it*,' said Eckels. 'I'm shaking like a kid.'

'Ah,' said Travis.

Everyone stopped.

Travis raised his hand. 'Ahead,' he whispered. 'In the mist. There he is. There's His Royal Majesty now.'

The jungle was wide and full of twitterings, rustlings, murmurs, and sighs.

Suddenly it all ceased, as if someone had shut a door.

Silence.

A sound of thunder.

Out of the mist, one hundred yards away, came *Tyrannosaurus rex*.

'No,' whispered Eckels. 'No. No.'

'Sh!'

It came on great oiled, resilient, striding legs. It towered thirty feet above half of the trees, a great evil god, folding its delicate watchmaker's claws, close to its oily reptilian chest. Each lower leg was a piston, a thousand pounds of white bone, sunk in thick ropes of muscle, sheathed over in a gleam of pebbled skin like the mail of a terrible warrior. Each thigh was a ton of meat, ivory, and steel mesh. And from the great breathing cage of the upper body those two delicate arms dangled out front, arms with hands which might pick up and examine men like toys, while the snake neck coiled. And the head itself, a ton of sculptured stone, lifted easily upon the sky. Its mouth gaped, exposing a fence of teeth like daggers. Its eyes rolled, ostrich eggs, empty of all expression save hunger. It closed its mouth in a death grin. It ran, its pelvic bones crushing aside trees and bushes, its taloned feet clawing damp earth, leaving prints six inches deep wherever it settled its weight. It ran with a gliding ballet step, far too poised and balanced for its ten tons. It moved into a sunlit arena warily, its beautifully reptile hands feeling the air.

'My God!' Eckels twitched his mouth. 'It could reach up and grab the moon.'

'Sh!' Travis jerked angrily. 'He hasn't seen us yet.'

'It can't be killed.' Eckels pronounced this verdict quietly, as if there could be no argument. He had weighed the evidence and this was his considered opinion. The rifle in his hands seemed a cap gun. 'We were fools to come. This is impossible.'

'Shut up!' hissed Travis.

'Nightmare.'

'Turn around,' commanded Travis. 'Walk quietly to the Machine. We'll remit one half your fee.'

'I didn't realize it would be this *big*,' said Eckels. 'I miscaluated, that's all. And now I want out.'

'It *sees* us!'

'There's the red paint on its chest!'

The Thunder Lizard raised itself. Its armoured flesh glittered like a thousand green coins. The coins, crusted with slime, steamed. In the slime, tiny insects wriggled, so that the entire body seemed to twitch and undulate, even while the monster itself did not move. It exhaled. The stink of raw flesh blew down the wilderness.

'Get me out of here,' said Eckels. 'It was never like this before. I was always sure I'd come through alive. I had good guides, good safaris, and safety. This time, I figured wrong. I've met my match and admit it. This is too much for me to get hold of.'

'Don't run,' said Lesperance. 'Turn around. Hide in the Machine.'

'Yes.' Eckels seemed to be numb. He looked at his feet as if trying to make them move. He gave a grunt of helplessness.

'Eckels!'

He took a few steps, blinking, shuffling.

'Not *that* way!'

The Monster, at the first motion, lunged forward with a terrible scream. It covered one hundred yards in four seconds. The rifles jerked up and blazed fire. A windstorm from the beast's mouth engulfed them in the stench of slime and old blood. The Monster roared, teeth glittering with sun.

Eckels, not looking back, walked blindly to the edge of the Path, his gun limp in his arms, stepped off the Path, and walked, not knowing it, in the jungle. His feet sank into green moss. His legs moved him, and he felt alone and remote from the events behind.

The rifles cracked again. Their sound was lost in shriek and lizard thunder. The great lever of the reptile's tail swung up, lashed sideways. Trees exploded in clouds of leaf and branch. The Monster twitched its jeweller's hands down to fondle at the men, to twist them in half, to crush them like berries, to cram them into its teeth and its screaming throat. Its boulder-stone eyes levelled with the men. They saw themselves mirrored. They fired at the metallic eyelids and the blazing black iris.

Like a stone idol, like a mountain avalanche, *Tyrannosaurus* fell. Thundering, it clutched trees, pulled them with it. It wrenched and tore the metal Path. The men flung themselves back and away. The body hit, ten tons of cold flesh and stone. The guns fired. The Monster lashed its armoured tail, twitched its snake jaws, and lay still. A fount of blood spurted from its throat. Somewhere inside, a sac of fluids burst. Sickening gushes drenched the hunters. They stood, red and glistening.

The thunder faded.

The jungle was silent. After the avalanche, a green peace. After the nightmare, morning.

Billings and Kramer sat on the pathway and threw up.

Travis and Lesperance stood with smoking rifles, cursing steadily.

In the Time Machine, on his face, Eckels lay shivering. He had found his way back to the Path, climbed into the Machine.

Travis came walking, glanced at Eckels, took cotton gauze from a metal box, and returned to the others, who were sitting on the Path.

'Clean up.'

They wiped the blood from their helmets. They began to curse too. The Monster lay, a hill of solid flesh. Within, you could hear the sighs and murmurs as the furthest chambers of it died, the organs malfunctioning, liquids running a final instant from pocket to sac to spleen, everything shutting off, closing up forever. It was like standing by a wrecked locomotive or a steam shovel at quitting time, all valves being released or levered tight. Bones cracked; the tonnage of its own flesh, off balance, dead weight, snapped the delicate forearms, caught underneath. The meat settled, quivering.

Another cracking sound. Overhead, a gigantic tree branch broke from its heavy mooring, fell. It crashed upon the dead beast with finality.

'There.' Lesperance checked his watch. 'Right on time. That's the giant tree that was scheduled to fall and kill this animal originally.' He glanced at the two hunters. 'You want the trophy picture?'

'What?'

'We can't take a trophy back to the Future. The body has to stay right here where it would have died originally, so the insects, birds, and bacteria can get at it, as they were intended to. Everything in balance. The body stays. But we *can* take a picture of you standing near it.

The two men tried to think, but gave up, shaking their heads.

They let themselves be led along the metal Path. They

sank wearily into the Machine cushions. They gazed back at the ruined Monster, the stagnating mound, where already strange reptilian birds and golden insects were busy at the steaming armour.

A sound on the floor of the The Machine stiffened them. Eckels sat there, shivering.

'I'm sorry,' he said at last.

'Get up!' cried Travis.

Eckels got up.

'Go out on that Path alone,' said Travis. He had his rifle pointed. 'You're not coming back in the Machine. We're leaving you here!'

Lesperance seized Travis's arm. 'Wait——'

'Stay out of this!' Travis shook his hand away. 'This idiot nearly killed us. But it isn't *that* so much, no. It's his *shoes*! Look at them! He ran off the Path. That *ruins* us! Who knows how much we'll forfeit! Tens of thousands of dollars of insurance! We guarantee no one leaves the Path. He left it. Oh, the damn fool! I'll have to report to the government. They might revoke our licence to travel. God knows *what* he's done to Time, to History!'

'Take it easy, all he did was kick up some dirt.'

'How do we *know*?' cried Travis. 'We don't know anything! It's all a damn mystery! Get out there, Eckels!'

Eckels fumbled his shirt. 'I'll pay anything. A hundred thousand dollars!'

Travis glared at Eckel's cheque book and spat. 'Go out there. The Monster's next to the Path. Stick your arms up to your elbows in his mouth. Then you can come back with us.'

'That's unreasonable!'

'The Monster's dead, you fool. The bullets! The bullets can't be left behind. They don't belong in the Past; they might change something. Here's my knife. Dig them out!'

The jungle was alive again, full of the old tremorings

and bird cries. Eckels turned slowly to regard that primeval garbage dump, that hill of nightmares and terror. After a long time, like a sleepwalker, he shuffled out along the Path.

He returned, shuddering, five minutes later, his arms soaked and red to the elbows. He held out his hands. Each held a number of steel bullets. Then he fell. He lay where he fell, not moving.

'You didn't have to make him do that,' said Lesperance.

'Didn't I? It's too early to tell.' Travis nudged the still body. 'He'll live. Next time he won't go hunting game like this. Okay.' He jerked his thumb wearily at Lesperance. 'Switch on. Let's go home.'

1492. 1776. 1812.

They cleaned their hands and faces. They changed their caking shirts and pants. Eckels was up and around again, not speaking. Travis glared at him for a full ten minutes.

'Don't look at me,' cried Eckels. 'I haven't done anything.'

'Who can tell?'

'Just ran off the Path, that's all, a little mud on my shoes —what do you want me to do—get down and pray?'

'We might need it. I'm warning you, Eckels, I might kill you yet. I've got my gun ready.'

'I'm innocent. I've done nothing!'

1999. 2000. 2055.

The Machine stopped.

'Get out,' Travis said.

The room was there as they had left it. But not the same as they had left it. The same man sat behind the same desk. But the same man did not quite sit behind the same desk.

Travis looked around swiftly. 'Everything okay here?' he snapped.

'Fine. Welcome home!'

Travis did not relax. He seemed to be looking at the very

atoms of the air itself, at the way the sun poured through the one high window.

'Okay, Eckels, get out. Don't ever come back.'

Eckels could not move.

'You heard me,' said Travis. 'What're you *staring* at?'

Eckels stood smelling of the air, and there was a thing to the air, a chemical taint so subtle, so slight, that only a faint cry of his sublimal senses warned him it was there. The colours, white, grey, blue, orange, in the wall, in the furniture, in the sky beyond the window, were . . . were . . . And there was a *feel*. His flesh twitched. His hands twitched. He stood drinking the oddness with the pores of his body. Somewhere, someone must have been screaming one of those whistles that only a dog can hear. His body screamed silence in return. Beyond this room, beyond this wall, beyond this man who was not quite the same man seated at this desk that was not quite the same desk . . . lay an entire world of streets and people. What sort of world it was now, there was no telling. He could feel them moving there, beyond the walls, almost, like so many chess pieces blown in a dry wind . . .

But the immediate thing was the sign painted on the office wall, the same sign he had read earlier today on first entering.

Somehow, the sign had changed:

> TYME SEFARI INC.
> SEFARIS TU ANY YEER EN THE PAST.
> YU NAIM THE ANIMALL.
> WEE TAEK YU THAIR.
> YU SHOOT ITT.

Eckels felt himself fall into a chair. He fumbled crazily at the thick slime on his boots. He held up a clod of dirt, trembling. 'No, it *can't* be. Not a *little* thing like that. No!'

Embedded in the mud, glistening green and gold and black, was a butterfly, very beautiful and very dead.

'Not a little thing like *that!* Not a butterfly!' cried Eckels.

F

It fell to the floor, an exquisite thing, a small thing that could upset balances and knock down a line of small dominoes and then big dominoes and then gigantic dominoes, all down the years across Time. Eckels' mind whirled. It *couldn't* change things. Killing one butterfly couldn't be *that* important! Could it?

His face was cold. His mouth trembled, asking: 'Who—who won the presidential election yesterday?'

The man behind the desk laughed. 'You joking? You know damn well. Deutscher, of course! Who else? Not that damn weakling Keith. We got an iron man now, a man with guts, by God!' The official stopped. 'What's wrong?'

Eckels moaned. He dropped to his knees. He scrabbled at the golden butterfly with shaking fingers. 'Can't we,' he pleaded to the world, to himself, to the officials, to the Machine, 'can't we take *it* back, can't we *make* it alive again? Can't we start over? Can't we——'

He did not move. Eyes shut, he waited, shivering. He heard Travis breathe loud in the room; he heard Travis shift his rifle, click the safety catch, and raise the weapon.

There was a sound of thunder.

HE WALKED AROUND THE HORSES

H. BEAM PIPER

IN NOVEMBER, 1809, an Englishman named Benjamin Bathurst vanished, inexplicably and utterly.

He was *en route* to Hamburg from Vienna, where he had been serving as his Government's envoy to the court of what Napoleon had left of the Austrian Empire. At an inn in Perleburg, in Prussia, while examining a change of horses for his coach, he casually stepped out of sight of his secretary and his valet. He was not seen to leave the inn-yard. He was not seen again, ever.

At least, not in this continuum . . .

I

(From Baron Eugen von Krutz, Minister of Police, to His Excellency the Count von Berchtenwald, Chancellor to His Majesty Freidrich Wilhelm III of Prussia.)

26 November, 1809.

Your Excellency:

A circumstance has come to the notice of this Ministry, the significance of which I am at a loss to define, but, since it appears to involve matters of state, both here and abroad, I am convinced that it is of sufficient importance to be brought to the personal attention of your Excellency.

Frankly, I am unwilling to take any further action in the matter without your Excellency's advice.

Briefly, the situation is this : We are holding, here at the Ministry of Police, a person giving his name as Benjamin Bathurst, who claims to be a British diplomat. This person was taken into custody by the police at Perleburg yesterday, as a result of a disturbance at an inn there; he is being detained on technical charges of causing disorder in a public place, and of being a suspicious person. When arrested, he had in his possession a dispatch-case, containing a number of papers; these are of such an extraordinary nature that the local authorities declined to assume any responsibility beyond having the man sent here to Berlin.

After interviewing this person and examining his papers, I am, I must confess, in much the same position. This is not, I am convinced, any ordinary police matter; there is something very strange and disturbing here. The man's statements, taken alone, are so incredible as to justify the assumption that he is mad. I cannot, however, adopt this theory, in view of his demeanour, which is that of a man of perfect rationality, and because of the existence of these papers. The whole thing is mad; incomprehensible !

The papers in question accompany, along with copies of the various statements taken in Perleburg, and a personal letter to me from my nephew, Lieutenant Rudolph von Tarlburg. This last is deserving of your Excellency's particular attention; Lieutenant von Tarlburg is a very level-headed young officer, not at all inclined to be fanciful or imaginative. It would take a good deal to affect him as he describes.

The man calling himself Benjamin Bathurst is now lodged in an apartment here at the Ministry; he is being treated with every consideration, and, except for freedom of movement, accorded every privilege.

I am, most anxiously awaiting your Excellency's advice, etc., etc.,

KRUTZ.

II

(Report of Traugott Zeller, *Oberwachtmeister*, *Staatspolizei*, made at Perleburg, 25 November, 1809.)

At about ten minutes past two of the afternoon of Saturday, 25 November, while I was at the police station, there entered a man known to me as Franz Bauer, an inn-servant employed by Christian Hauck, at the sign of the Sword and Sceptre, here in Perleburg. This man Franz Bauer made complaint to Staatspolizeikapitän Ernst Hartenstein, saying that there was a madman making trouble at the inn where he, Franz Bauer, worked. I was therefore directed by Staatspolizeikapitän Hartenstein to go to the Sword and Sceptre Inn, there to act at discretion to maintain the peace.

Arriving at the inn in company with the said Franz Bauer, I found a considerable crowd of people in the common-room, and, in the midst of them, the innkeeper, Christian Hauck, in altercation with a stranger. This stranger was a gentlemanly-appearing person, dressed in travelling-clothes, who had under his arm a small leather dispatch-case. As I entered, I could hear him, speaking in German with a strong English accent, abusing the innkeeper, the said Christian Hauck, and accusing him of having drugged his, the stranger's, wine, and of having stolen his, the stranger's, coach-and-four, and of having abducted his, the stranger's, secretary and servants. This the said Christian Hauck was loudly denying, and the other people in the inn were taking the innkeeper's part, and mocking the stranger for a madman.

On entering, I commanded everyone to be silent, in the King's name, and then, as he appeared to be the complaining party of the dispute, I required the foreign gentleman to state to me what was the trouble. He then repeated his accusations against the innkeeper, Hauck, saying that Hauck, or rather, another man who resembled Hauck and who had claimed to be the innkeeper, had drugged his wine and stolen his coach and made off with his secretary and his servants. At this point, the innkeeper and the bystanders all began shouting denials and contradictions, so that I had to pound on a table with my truncheon to command silence.

I then required the innkeeper, Christian Hauck, to answer the charges which the stranger had made; this he did with a complete denial of all of them, saying that the stranger had had no wine in his inn, and that he had not been inside the inn until a few minutes before, when he had burst in shouting accusations, and that there had been no secretary, and no valet, and no coachman, and no coach-and-four, at the inn, and that the gentleman was raving mad. To all this, he called the people who were in the common-room to witness.

I then required the stranger to account for himself. He said that his name was Benjamin Bathurst, and that he was a British diplomat, returning to England from Vienna. To prove this, he produced from his dispatch-case sundry papers. One of these was a letter of safe-conduct, issued by the Prussian Chancellery, in which he was named and described as Benjamin Bathurst. The other papers were English, all bearing seals, and appearing to be official documents.

Accordingly, I requested him to accompany me to the police station, and also the innkeeper, and three men whom the innkeeper wanted to bring as witnesses.

TRAUGOTT ZELLER.
Oberwachtmeister.

Report approved,

ERNST HARTENSTEIN.
Staatspolizeikapitän.

III

(Statement of the self-so-called Benjamin Bathurst, taken at the police station at Perleburg, 25 November, 1809.)

My name is Benjamin Bathurst, and I am Envoy Extraordinary and Minister Plenipotentiary of the Government of His Britannic Majesty to the court of His Majesty Franz I, Emperor of Austria, or at least I was until the events following the Austrian surrender made necessary my return to London. I left Vienna on the morning of Monday, the 20th, to go to Hamburg to take ship home; I was travelling in my own coach-and-four, with my secretary, Mr. Bertram Jardine, and my valet, William Small, both British subjects, and a coachman, Josef Bidek, an Austrian subject, whom I had hired for the trip. Because of the presence of French troops, whom I was anxious to avoid, I was forced to make a detour west as far as Salzburg before turning north towards Magdeburg, where I crossed the Elbe. I was unable to get a change of horses for my coach after leaving Gera, until I reached Perleburg, where I stopped at the Sword and Sceptre Inn.

Arriving there, I left my coach in the inn-yard, and I and my secretary, Mr. Jardine, went into the inn. A man, not this fellow here, but another rogue, with more beard and less paunch, and more shabbily dressed, but as like him as though he were his brother, represented himself as the innkeeper, and I dealt with him for a change of horses, and ordered a bottle of wine for myself and my secretary, and also a pot of beer apiece for my valet and the coachman, to be taken outside to them. Then Jardine and I sat down to our wine, at a table in the common-room, until the man who claimed to be the innkeeper came back and told us that the fresh horses were harnessed to the coach and ready to go. Then we went outside again.

I looked at the two horses on the off-side, and then

walked around in front of the team to look at the two nigh-side horses, and as I did, I felt giddy, as though I were about to fall, and everything went black before my eyes. I thought I was having a fainting-spell, something I am not at all subject to, and I put out my hand to grasp the hitching-bar, but could not find it. I am sure, now, that I was unconscious for some time, because when my head cleared, the coach and horses were gone, and in their place was a big farm-wagon, jacked up in front, with the right wheel off, and two peasants were greasing the detached wheel.

I looked at them for a moment, unable to credit my eyes, and then I spoke to them in German, saying, 'Where the devil's my coach-and-four?'

They both straightened, startled; the one who was holding the wheel almost dropped it.

'Pardon, Excellency,' he said. 'There's been no coach-and-four here, all the time we've been here.'

'Yes,' said his mate, 'and we've been here since just after noon.'

I did not attempt to argue with them. It occurred to me —and it is still my opinion—that I was the victim of some plot; that my wine had been drugged, that I had been unconscious for some time during which my coach had been removed and this wagon substituted for it, and that these peasants had been put to work on it and instructed what to say if questioned. If my arrival at the inn had been anticipated, and everything put in readiness, the whole business would not have taken ten minutes.

I therefore entered the inn, determined to have it out with this rascally innkeeper, but when I returned to the common-room, he was nowhere to be seen, and this other fellow, who has also given his name as Christian Hauck, claimed to be the innkeeper and denied knowledge of any of the things I have just stated. Furthermore, there were four cavalrymen, Uhlans, drinking beer and playing cards at the table where Jardine and I had had our wine, and they claimed to have been there for several hours.

I have no idea why such an elaborate prank, involving the participation of many people, should be played on me, except at the instigation of the French. In that case, I cannot understand why Prussian soldiers should lend themselves to it.

BENJAMIN BATHURST.

IV

(Statement of Christian Hauck, innkeeper, taken at the police station at Perleburg, 25 November, 1809.)

May it please your Honour, my name is Christian Hauck, and I keep an inn at the sign of the Sword and Sceptre, and have these past fifteen years, and my father, and his father, before him, for the past fifty years, and never has there been a complaint like this against my inn. Your Honour, it is a hard thing for a man who keeps a decent house, and pays his taxes, and obeys the laws, to be accused of crimes of this sort.

I know nothing of this gentleman, nor of his coach nor his secretary nor his servants; I never set eyes on him before he came bursting into the inn from the yard, shouting and raving like a madman, and crying out, 'Where the devil's that rogue of an innkeeper?'

I said to him, 'I am the innkeeper; what cause have you to call me a rogue, sir?'

The stranger replied:

'You're not the innkeeper I did business with a few minutes ago, and he's the rascal I have a row to pick with. I want to know what the devil's been done with my coach, and what's happened to my secretary and my servants.'

I tried to tell him that I knew nothing of what he was talking about, but he would not listen, and gave me the lie, saying that he had been drugged and robbed, and his people kidnapped. He even had the impudence to claim that he and his secretary had been sitting at a table in that room, drinking wine, not fifteen minutes before, when there had been four non-commissioned officers of the Third Uhlans at that table since noon. Everybody in the room spoke up for me, but he would not listen, and was shouting that we were all robbers, kidnappers, and French spies, and I don't know what all, when the police came.

Your Honour, the man is mad. What I have told you about this is the truth, and all that I know about this business, so help me God.

CHRISTIAN HAUCK.

V

(Statement of Franz Bauer, inn-servant, taken at the police station at Perleburg, 25 November, 1809.)

May it please your Honour, my name is Franz Bauer, and I am a servant at the Sword and Sceptre Inn, kept by Christian Hauck.

This afternoon, when I went into the inn-yard to empty a bucket of slops on the dung-heap by the stables, I heard voices and turned around, to see this gentleman speaking to Wilhelm Beick and Fritz Herzer, who were greasing their wagon in the yard. He had not been in the yard when I had turned around to empty the bucket, and I thought that he must have come in from the street. This gentleman was asking Beick and Herzer where was his coach, and when they told him they didn't know, he turned and ran into the inn.

Of my own knowledge, the man had not been inside the inn before then, nor had there been any coach, or any of the people he spoke of, at the inn, and none of the things he spoke of happened there, for otherwise I would know, since I was at the inn all day.

When I went back inside, I found him in the common-room, shouting at my master, and claiming that he had been drugged and robbed. I saw that he was mad, and was afraid that he would do some mischief, so I went for the police.

FRANZ BAUER
his (X) mark.

VI

(Statements of Wilhelm Beick and Fritz Herzer, peasants, taken at the police station at Perleburg, 25 November, 1809.)

May it please your Honour, my name is Wilhelm Beick, and I am a tenant on the estate of the Baron von Hentig. On this day, I and Fritz Herzer were sent in to Perleburg with a load of potatoes and cabbages which the innkeeper at the Sword and Sceptre had bought from the estate-superintendent. After we had unloaded them, we decided to grease our wagon, which was very dry, before going back, so we unhitched and began working on it. We took about two hours, starting just after we had eaten lunch, and in all that time there was no coach-and-four in the inn-yard. We were just finishing when this gentleman spoke to us, demanding to know where his coach was. We told him that there had been no coach in the yard all the time we had been there, so he turned around and ran into the inn. At the time, I thought that he had come out of the inn before speaking to us, for I know that he could not have come in from the street. Now I do not know where he came from, but I know that I never saw him before that moment.

WILHELM BEICK
his (X) mark.

I have heard the above testimony, and it is true to my own knowledge, and I have nothing to add to it.

FRITZ HERZER
his (X) mark.

VII

(From Staatspolizeikapitän Ernst Hartenstein, to His Excellency, the Baron von Krutz, Minister of Police.)

25 November, 1809.

Your Excellency:

The accompanying copies of statements taken this day will explain how the prisoner, the self-so-called Benjamin Bathurst, came into my custody. I have charged him with causing disorder and being a suspicious person, to hold him until more can be learned about him. However, as he represents himself to be a British diplomat, I am unwilling to assume any further responsibility, and am having him sent to your Excellency, in Berlin.

In the first place, your Excellency, I have the strongest doubts of the man's story. The statement which he made before me, and signed, is bad enough, with a coach-and-four turning into a farm-wagon, like Cinderella's coach into a pumpkin, and three people vanishing as though swallowed by the earth. Your Excellency will permit me to doubt that there ever was any such coach, or any such people. But all this is perfectly reasonable and credible, beside the things he said to me, of which no record was made.

Your Excellency will have noticed, in his statement, certain allusions to the Austrian surrender, and to French troops in Austria. After his statement had been taken down, I noticed these allusions, and I inquired, what surrender, and what were French troops doing in Austria. The man looked at me in a pitying manner, and said:

'News seems to travel slowly, hereabouts; peace was concluded at Vienna on the 14th of last month. And as for what French troops are doing in Austria, they're doing the same things Bonaparte's brigands are doing everywhere in Europe.'

'And who is Bonaparte?' I asked.

He stared at me as though I had asked him, 'Who is the Lord Jehovah?' Then, after a moment, a look of comprehension came into his face.

'So; you Prussians conceded him the title of Emperor, and refer to him as Napoleon,' he said, 'Well, I can assure you that His Britannic Majesty's Government haven't done so, and never will; not so long as one Englishman has a finger left to pull a trigger. General Bonaparte is a usurper; His Britannic Majesty's Government do not recognize any sovereignty in France except the House of Bourbon.' This he said very sternly, as though rebuking me.

It took me a moment or so to digest that, and to appreciate all its implications. Why, this fellow evidently believed, as a matter of fact, that the French Monarchy had been overthrown by some military adventurer named Bonaparte, who was calling himself the Emperor Napoleon, and who had made war on Austria and forced a surrender. I made no attempt to argue with him—one wastes time arguing with madmen—but if this man could believe that, the transformation of a coach-and-four into a cabbage-wagon was a small matter indeed. So, to humour him, I asked him if he thought General Bonaparte's agents were responsible for his trouble at the inn.

'Certainly,' he replied. 'The chances are they didn't know me to see me, and took Jardine for the Minister, and me for the secretary, so they made off with poor Jardine. I wonder, though, that they left me my dispatch-case. And that reminds me: I'll want that back. Diplomatic papers, you know.'

I told him, very seriously, that we would have to check his credentials. I promised him I would make every effort to locate his secretary and his servants and his coach, took a complete description of all of them, and persuaded him to go into an upstairs room, where I kept him under guard. I did start inquiries, calling in all my informers and spies, but, as I expected, I could learn nothing. I could not find

anybody, even, who had seen him anywhere in Perleburg
before he appeared at the Sword and Sceptre, and that
rather surprised me, as somebody should have seen him
enter the town, or walk along the street.

In this connection, let me remind your Excellency of
the discrepancy in the statements of the servant, Franz
Bauer, and of the two peasants. The former is certain the
man entered the inn-yard from the street; the latter are just
as positive that he did not. Your Excellency, I do not like
such puzzles, for I am sure that all three were telling the
truth to the best of their knowledge. They are ignorant
common-folk, I admit, but they should know what they
did or did not see.

After I got the prisoner into safe-keeping, I fell to examining his papers, and I can assure your Excellency that they
gave me a shock. I had paid little heed to his ravings about
the King of France being dethroned, or about this General
Bonaparte who called himself the Emperor Napoleon, but I
found all these things mentioned in his papers and dispatches, which had every appearance of being official documents. There was repeated mention of the taking, by the
French, of Vienna, last May, and of the capitulation of the
Austrian Emperor to this General Bonaparte, and of battles
being fought all over Europe, and I don't know what other
fantastic things. Your Excellency, I have heard of all sorts
of madmen—one believing himself to be the Archangel
Gabriel, or Mohammed, or a werewolf, and another convinced that his bones are made of glass, or that he is pursued and tormented by devils—but, so help me God, this is
the first time I have heard of a madman who had documentary proof for his delusions! Does your Excellency
wonder, then, that I want no part of this business?

But the matter of his credentials was even worse. He
had papers, sealed with the seal of the British Foreign Office,
and to every appearance genuine—but they were signed,
as Foreign Minister, by one George Canning, and all the
world knows that Lord Castlereagh has been Foreign Min-

ister these last five years. And to cap it all, he had a safe-conduct, sealed with the seal of the Prussian Chancellery —the very seal, for I compared it, under a strong magnifying-glass, with one that I knew to be genuine, and they were identical!—and yet, this letter was signed, as Chancellor, not by Count von Berchtenwald, but by Baron vom und zum Stein, the Minister of Agriculture, and the signature, as far as I could see, appeared to be genuine! This is too much for me, your Excellency; I must ask to be excused from dealing with this matter, before I become as mad as my prisoner!

I made arrangements, accordingly, with Colonel Keitel, of the Third Uhlans, to furnish an officer to escort this man in to Berlin. The coach in which they come belongs to this police station, and the driver is one of my men. He should be furnished expense-money to get back to Perleburg. The guard is a corporal of Uhlans, the orderly of the officer. He will stay with the *Herr Oberleutnant*, and both of them will return here at their own convenience and expense.

I have the honour, your Excellency, to be, etc., etc.,

ERNST HARTENSTEIN.
Staatspolizeikapitän.

VIII

(From Oberleutnant Rudolf von Tarlburg, to Baron Eugen von Krutz.)

26 November, 1809.

Dear Uncle Eugen:

This is in no sense a formal report; I made that at the Ministry, when I turned the Englishman and his papers over to one of your officers—a fellow with red hair and a face like a bulldog. But there are a few things which you should be told, which wouldn't look well in an official report, to let you know just what sort of a rare fish has got into your net.

I had just come in from drilling my platoon, yesterday, when Colonel Keitel's orderly told me that the colonel wanted to see me in his quarters. I found the old fellow in undress in his sitting-room, smoking his big pipe.

'Come in, Lieutenant; come in and sit down, my boy!' he greeted me, in that bluff, hearty manner which he always adopts with his junior officers when he has some particularly nasty job to be done. 'How would you like to take a little trip in to Berlin? I have an errand, which won't take half an hour, and you can stay as long as you like, just so you're back by Thursday, when your turn comes up for road-patrol.'

Well, I thought, this is the bait. I waited to see what the hook would look like, saying that it was entirely agreeable with me, and asking what his errand was.

'Well, it isn't for myself, Tarlburg,' he said. 'It's for this fellow Hartenstein, the *Staatspolizeikapitän* here. He has something he wants done at the Ministry of Police, and I thought of you because I've heard you're related to the Baron von Krutz. You are, aren't you?' he asked, just as though he didn't know all about who all his officers are related to.

'That's right, Colonel; the Baron is my uncle,' I said. 'What does Hartenstein want done?'

'Why, he has a prisoner whom he wants taken to Berlin and turned over at the Ministry. All you have to do is to take him in, in a coach, and see he doesn't escape on the way, and get a receipt for him, and for some papers. This is a very important prisoner; I don't think Hartenstein has anybody he can trust to handle him. A state prisoner. He claims to be some sort of a British diplomat, and for all Hartenstein knows, maybe he is. Also, he is a madman.'

'A madman?' I echoed.

'Yes, just so. At least, that's what Hartenstein told me. I wanted to know what sort of a madman—there are various kinds of madmen, all of whom must be handled differently—but all Hartenstein would tell me was that he had unrealistic beliefs about the state of affairs in Europe.'

'Ha! What diplomat hasn't?' I asked.

Old Keitel gave a laugh, somewhere between the bark of a dog and the croaking of a raven.

'Yes, naturally! The unrealistic beliefs of diplomats are what soldiers die of,' he said. 'I said as much to Hartenstein, but he wouldn't tell me anything more. He seemed to regret having said even that much. He looked like a man who's seen a particularly terrifying ghost.' The old man puffed hard at his famous pipe for a while, blowing smoke up through his moustache. 'Rudi, Hartenstein has pulled a hot potato out of the ashes, this time, and he wants to toss it to your uncle, before he burns his fingers. I think that's one reason why he got me to furnish an escort for his Englishman. Now, look; you must take this unrealistic diplomat, or this undiplomatic madman, or whatever in blazes he is, in to Berlin. And understand this.' He pointed his pipe at me as though it were a pistol. 'Your orders are to take him there and turn him over at the Ministry of Police. Nothing has been said about whether you turn him over alive or dead, or half one and half the other. I know nothing about this business, and want to know nothing; if Hartenstein wants us to play gaol-warders for him, then, *bei Gott*, he must be satisfied with our way of doing it!'

Well, to cut short the story, I looked at the coach Hartenstein had placed at my disposal, and I decided to chain the left door shut on the outside so that it couldn't be opened from within. Then, I would put my prisoner on my left, so that the only way out would be past me. I decided not to carry any weapons which he might be able to snatch from me, so I took off my sabre and locked it in the seat-box, along with the dispatch-case containing the Englishman's papers. It was cold enough to wear a greatcoat in comfort, so I wore mine, and in the right side pocket, where my prisoner couldn't reach, I put a little leaded bludgeon, and also a brace of pocket-pistols. Hartenstein

G

was going to furnish me a guard as well as a driver, but I said that I would take a servant who could act as guard. The servant, of course, was my orderly, old Johann; I gave him my double hunting-gun to carry, with a big charge of boar-shot in one barrel and an ounce ball in the other.

In addition, I armed myself with a big bottle of cognac. I thought that if I could shoot my prisoner often enough with that, he would give me no trouble.

As it happened, he didn't, and none of my precautions—except the cognac—were needed. The man didn't look like a lunatic to me. He was a rather stout gentleman, of past middle age, with a ruddy complexion and an intelligent face. The only unusual thing about him was his hat, which was a peculiar contraption, looking like the pot out of a close-stool. I put him in the carriage, and then offered him a drink out of my bottle, taking one about half as big myself. He smacked his lips over it and said, 'Well, that's real brandy; whatever we think of their detestable politics, we can't criticize the French for their liquor.' Then, he said, 'I'm glad they're sending me in the custody of a military gentleman, instead of a confounded gendarme. Tell me the truth, Lieutenant: am I under arrest for anything?'

'Why,' I said, 'Captain Hartenstein should have told you about that. All I know is that I have orders to take you to the Ministry of Police, in Berlin, and not to let you escape on the way. These orders I will carry out; I hope you don't hold that against me.'

He assured me that he did not, and we had another drink on it—I made sure, again, that he got twice as much as I did—and then the coachman cracked his whip and we were off for Berlin.

Now, I thought, I am going to see just what sort of a madman this is, and why Hartenstein is making a state affair out of a squabble at an inn. So I decided to explore his unrealistic beliefs about the state of affairs in Europe.

After guiding the conversation to where I wanted it, I asked him:

'What, Herr Bathurst, in your belief, is the real, under-lying cause of the present tragic situation in Europe?'

That, I thought, was safe enough. Name me one year, since the days of Julius Caesar, when the situation in Europe hasn't been tragic! And it worked, to perfection.

'In my belief,' says this Englishman, 'the whole damnable mess is the result of the victory of the rebellious colonists in North America, and their blasted republic.'

Well, you can imagine, that gave me a start. All the world knows that the American Patriots lost their war for independence from England; that their army was shattered, that their leaders were either killed or driven into exile. How many times, when I was a little boy, did I not sit up long past my bedtime, when old Baron von Steuben was a guest at Tarlburg-Schloss, listening open-mouthed and wide-eyed to his stories of that gallant lost struggle! How I used to shiver at his tales of the terrible Winter camp, or thrill at the battles, or weep as he told how he held the dying Washington in his arms, and listened to his noble last words, at the Battle of Doylestown! And here, this man was telling me that the Patriots had really won, and set up the republic for which they had fought! I had been pre-pared for some of what Hartenstein had called unrealistic beliefs, but nothing as fantastic as this.

'I can cut it even finer than that,' Bathurst continued. 'It was the defeat of Burgoyne at Saratoga. We made a good bargain when we got Benedict Arnold to turn his coat, but we didn't do it soon enough. If he hadn't been on the field that day, Burgoyne would have gone through Gates's army like a hot knife through butter.'

But Arnold hadn't been at Saratoga, I know; I have read much of the American War. Arnold was shot dead on New Year's Day of 1776, during the attempted storming of Quebec. And Burgoyne had done just as Bathurst had said: he had gone through Gates like a knife, and down the Hudson to join Howe.

'But, Herr Bathurst,' I asked, 'how could that affect the

situation in Europe? America is thousands of miles away, across the ocean.'

'Ideas can cross oceans quicker than armies. When Louis XVI decided to come to the aid of the Americans, he doomed himself and his régime. A successful resistance to royal authority in America was all the French Republicans needed to inspire them. Of course, we have Louis's own weakness to blame, too. If he'd given those rascals a whiff of grapeshot when the mob tried to storm Versailles in 1790 there'd have been no French Revolution.'

But he had. When Louis XVI ordered the howitzers turned on the mob at Versailles, and then sent the dragoons to ride down the survivors, the Republican movement had been broken. That had been when Cardinal Talleyrand, who had then been merely Bishop of Autun, had come to the fore and became the power that he is today in France; the greatest King's Minister since Richelieu.

'And, after that, Louis's death followed as surely as night after day,' Bathurst was saying. 'And because the French had no experience in self-government, their republic was foredoomed. If Bonaparte hadn't seized power, somebody else would have; when the French murdered their king, they delivered themselves to dictatorship. And a dictator, unsupported by the prestige of royalty, has no choice but to lead his people into foreign war, to keep them from turning upon him.'

It was like that all the way to Berlin. All these things seem foolish by daylight, but as I sat in the darkness of that swaying coach, I was almost convinced of the reality of what he told me. I tell you, Uncle Eugen, it was frightening, as though he were giving me a view of Hell. *Gott in Himmel*, the things that man talked of! Armies swarming over Europe; sack and massacre, and cities burning; blockades, and starvation; kings deposed, and thrones tumbling like tenpins! Battles in which the soldiers of every nation fought, and in which tens of thousands were mowed down like ripe grain; and, over all, the Satanic figure of a little man in a grey coat, who dictated peace to the Austrian Emperor in Schoenbrunn, and carried the Pope away a prisoner to Savona.

Madman, eh? Unrealistic beliefs, says Hartenstein? Well, give me madmen who drool spittle, and foam at the mouth, and shriek obscene blasphemies. But not this pleasant-seeming gentleman who sat beside me and talked of horrors in a quiet, cultured voice, while he drank my cognac.

But not all my cognac! If your man at the Ministry —the one with red hair and the bulldog face—tells you that I was drunk when I brought in that Englishman, you had better believe him!

RUDI.

IX

(From Count von Berchtenwald to the British Minister.)

28 November, 1809.

Honoured Sir:

The accompanying *dossier* will acquaint you with the problem confronting this Chancellery, without needless repetition on my part. Please to understand that it is not, and never was, any part of the intentions of the Government of His Majesty Friedrich Wilhelm III to offer any injury or indignity to the Government of His Britannic Majesty George III. We would never contemplate holding in arrest the person, or tampering with the papers, of an accredited envoy of your Government. However, we have the gravest doubt, to make a considerable understatement, that this person who calls himself Benjamin Bathurst is any such envoy, and we do not think that it would be any service to the Government of His Britannic Majesty to allow an impostor to travel about Europe in the guise of a British diplomatic representative. We certainly should not thank the Government of His Britannic Majesty for failing to take steps to deal with some person who, in England, might falsely represent himself to be a Prussian diplomat.

This affair touches us almost as closely as it does your own Government; this man had in his possession a letter of safe conduct, which you will find in the accompanying dispatch-case. It is of the regular form, as issued by this Chancellery, and is sealed with the Chancellery seal, or with a very exact counterfeit of it. However, it has been signed, as Chancellor of Prussia, with a signature indistinguishable from that of the Baron vom und zum Stein, who is the present Minister of Agriculture. Baron Stein was shown the signature, with the rest of the letter covered, and without hesitation acknowledged it for his own writing. However, when the letter was uncovered and shown to him, his surprise and horror were such as would require the pen of a Goethe or a Schiller to describe, and he denied categorically ever having seen the document before.

I have no choice but to believe him. It is impossible to think that a man of Baron Stein's honourable and serious character would be party to the fabrication of a paper of this sort. Even aside from this, I am in the thing as deeply as he; if it is signed with his signature, it is also sealed with my seal, which has not been out of my personal keeping in the ten years that I have been Chancellor here. In fact, the word 'impossible' can be used to describe the entire business. It was impossible for the man Benjamin Bathurst to have entered the inn-yard—yet he did. It was impossible that he should carry papers of the sort found in his dispatch-case, or that such papers should exist—yet I am sending them to you with this letter. It is impossible that Baron vom und zum Stein should sign a paper of the sort he did, or that it should be sealed by the Chancellery —yet it bears both Stein's signature and my seal.

You will also find in the dispatch-case other credentials ostensibly originating with the British Foreign Office of the same character, being signed by persons having no connection with the Foreign Office, or even with the Government, but being sealed with apparently authentic seals. If you send these papers to London, I fancy you will find that they will there create the same situation as that caused here by this letter of safe-conduct.

I am also sending you a charcoal sketch of the person who calls himself Benjamin Bathurst. This portrait was taken without its subject's knowledge. Baron von Krutz's nephew, Lieutenant von Tarlburg, who is the son of our mutual friend Count von Tarlburg, has a *little friend*, a very clever young lady who is, as you will see, an expert at this sort of work; she was introduced into a room at the Ministry of Police and placed behind a screen, where she could sketch our prisoner's face. If you should send this picture to London, I think that there is a good chance that it might be recognized. I can vouch that it is an excellent likeness.

To tell the truth, we are at our wits' end about this affair. I cannot understand how such excellent imitations of these various seals could be made, and the signature of the Baron vom und zum Stein is the most expert forgery that I have ever seen, in thirty years' experience as a statesman. This would indicate careful and painstaking work on the part of somebody; how, then, do we reconcile this with such clumsy mistakes, recognizable as such by any schoolboy, as signing the name of Baron Stein as Prussian Chancellor, or Mr. George Canning, who is a member of the opposition party and not connected with your Government, as British Foreign Secretary?

These are mistakes which only a madman would make. There are those who think our prisoner is a madman, because of his apparent delusions about the great conqueror, General Bonaparte, *alias* the Emperor Napoleon. Madmen have been known to fabricate evidence to support their delusions, it is true, but I shudder to think of a madman having at his disposal the resources to manufacture the papers you will find in this dispatch-case. Moreover, some of our foremost medical men, who have specialized in the disorders of the mind, have interviewed this man Bathurst and say that, save for his fixed belief in a non-existent situation, he is perfectly rational.

Personally, I believe that the whole thing is a gigantic hoax, perpetrated for some hidden and sinister purpose, possibly to create confusion, and undermine the confidence existing between your Government and mine, and to set against one another various persons connected with both Governments, or else as a mask for some other conspiratorial activity. Without specifying any Sovereigns or Governments who might wish to do this, I can think of two groups, namely, the Jesuits, and the outlawed French Republicans, either of whom might conceive such a situation to be to their advantage. Only a few months ago, you will recall, there was a Jacobin plot unmasked at Köln.

But, whatever this business may portend, I do not like it. I want to get to the bottom of it as soon as possible, and I will thank you, my dear Sir, and your Government, for any assistance you may find possible.

I have the honour, Sir, to be, etc., etc., etc.,

BERCHTENWALD.

X

FROM BARON VON KRUTZ, TO THE COUNT VON BERCHTENWALD.
MOST URGENT; MOST IMPORTANT.
TO BE DELIVERED IMMEDIATELY AND IN PERSON, REGARDLESS OF CIRCUMSTANCES.

28 November, 1809.

Count von Berchtenwald:

Within the past half-hour, that is, at about eleven o'clock tonight, the man calling himself Benjamin Bathurst was shot and killed by a sentry at the Ministry of Police, while attempting to escape from custody.

A sentry on duty in the rear courtyard of the Ministry

observed a man attempting to leave the building in a suspicious and furtive manner. This sentry, who was under the strictest orders to allow no one to enter or leave without written authorization, challenged him; when he attempted to run, the sentry fired his musket at him, bringing him down. At the shot, the Sergeant of the Guard rushed into the courtyard with his detail, and the man whom the sentry had shot was found to be the Englishman, Benjamin Bathurst. He had been hit in the chest with an ounce ball, and died before the doctor could arrive, and without recovering consciousness.

An investigation revealed that the prisoner, who was confined on the third floor of the building, had fashioned a rope from his bedding, his bed-cord, and the leather strap of his bell-pull; this rope was only long enough to reach to the window of the office on the second floor, directly below, but he managed to enter this by kicking the glass out of the window. I am trying to find out how he could do this without being heard; I can assure your Excellency that somebody is going to smart for this night's work. As for the sentry, he acted within his orders; I have commended him for doing his duty, and for good shooting, and I assume full responsibility for the death of the prisoner at his hands.

I have no idea why the self-so-called Benjamin Bathurst, who, until now, was well behaved and seemed to take his confinement philosophically, should suddenly make this rash and fatal attempt, unless it was because of those infernal dunderheads of madhouse-doctors who have been bothering him. Only this afternoon, your Excellency, they deliberately handed him a bundle of newspapers—Prussian, Austrian, French, and English—all dated within the last month. They wanted, they said, to see how he would react. Well, God pardon them, they've found out!

What does your Excellency think should be done about giving the body burial?

KRUTZ.

(From the British Minister to the Count von Berchten-wald.)

December 20th, 1809.

My dear Count von Berchtenwald:

Reply from London to my letter of the 28th *ult.*, which accompanied the dispatch-case and the other papers, has finally come to hand. The papers which you wanted returned—the copies of the statements taken at Perleburg, the letter to the Baron von Krutz from the police captain, Hartenstein, and the personal letter of Krutz's nephew, Lieutenant von Tarlburg, and the letter of safe-conduct found in the dispatch-case, accompany herewith. I don't know what the people at Whitehall did with the other papers; tossed them into the nearest fire, for my guess. Were I in your Excellency's place, that's where the papers I am returning would go.

I have heard nothing yet, from my dispatch of the 29th *ult.* concerning the death of the man who called himself Benjamin Bathurst, but I doubt very much if any official notice will ever be taken of it. Your Government had a perfect right to detain the fellow, and, that being the case, he attemptcd to escape at his own risk. After all, sentries are not required to carry loaded muskets in order to discourage them from putting their hands in their pockets.

To hazard a purely unofficial opinion, I should not imagine that London is very much dissatisfied with this *dénouement*. His Majesty's Government are a hard-headed and matter-of-fact set of gentry who do not relish mysteries, least of all mysteries whose solution may be more disturbing than the original problem.

This is entirely confidential, your Excellency, but those papers which were in that dispatch-case kicked up the devil's own row in London, with half the Government big-wigs protesting their innocence to high Heaven, and the rest accusing one another of complicity in the hoax. If that was somebody's intention, it was literally a howling success. For a while, it was even feared that there would be Questions in Parliament, but eventually the whole vexatious business was hushed.

You may tell Count Tarlburg's son that his little friend is a most talented young lady; her sketch was highly commended by no less an authority than Sir Thomas Lawrence, and here, your Excellency, comes the most bedevilling part of a thoroughly bedevilled business. The picture was instantly recognized. It is a very fair likeness of Benjamin Bathurst, or, I should say, Sir Benjamin Bathurst, who is King's Lieutenant-Governor for the Crown Colony of Georgia. As Sir Thomas Lawrence did his portrait a few years back, he is in an excellent position to criticize the work of Lieutenant von Tarlburg's young lady. However, Sir Benjamin Bathurst was known to have been in Savannah, attending to the duties of his office, and in the public eye, all the while that his double was in Prussia. Sir Benjamin does not have a twin brother. It has been suggested that this fellow might be a half-brother, born on the wrong side of the blanket, but, as far as I know, there is no justification for this theory.

The General Bonaparte, alias the Emperor Napoleon, who is given so much mention in the dispatches, seems also to have counterpart in actual life; there is, in the French army, a Colonel of Artillery by that name, a Corsican who Gallicized his original name of Napolione Buonaparte. He is a most brilliant military theoretician; I am sure some of your officers, like General Scharnhorst, could tell you about him. His loyalty to the French Monarchy has never been questioned.

This same correspondence to fact seems to crop up everywhere in that amazing collection of pseudo-dispatches and pseudo-state-papers. The United States of America, you will recall, was the style by which the rebellious colonies referred to themselves, in the Declaration of Philadelphia. The James Madison who is mentioned as the current President of the United States, is now living, in exile, in Switzerland. His alleged predecessor in office, Thomas Jefferson, was the author of the rebel Declaration; after the defeat of the rebels, he escaped to Havana, and died, several years ago, in the Principality of Lichtenstein.

I was quite amused to find our old friend Cardinal Talleyrand—without the ecclesiastical title—cast in the role of chief adviser to the usurper, Bonaparte. His Eminence, I have always thought, is the sort of fellow who would land on his feet on top of any heap, and who would as little scruple to be Prime Minister to His Satanic Majesty as to His Most Christian Majesty.

I was baffled, however, by one name, frequently mentioned in those fantastic papers. This was the English General, Wellington. I haven't the least idea who this person might be.

I have the honour, your Excellency, etc., etc., etc.,

SIR ARTHUR WELLESLEY.

ZERO HOUR

RAY BRADBURY

OH, IT was to be so jolly! What a game! Such excitement they hadn't known in years. The children catapulted this way and that across the green lawns, shouting at each other, holding hands, flying in circles, climbing trees, laughing. Overhead the rockets flew, and beetle cars whispered by on the streets, but the children played on. Such fun, such tremulous joy, such tumbling and hearty screaming.

Mink ran into the house, all dirt and sweat. For her seven years she was loud and strong and definite. Her mother, Mrs. Morris, hardly saw her as she yanked out drawers and rattled pans and tools in to a large sack.

'Heavens, Mink, what's going on?'

'The most exciting game ever!' gasped Mink, pink-faced.

'Stop and get your breath,' said her mother.

'No, I'm all right,' gasped Mink. 'Okay I take these things, Mom?'

'But don't dent them,' said Mrs. Morris.

'Thank you, thank you!' cried Mink, and boom! she was gone, like a rocket.

Mrs. Morris surveyed the fleeing tot. 'What's the name of the game?'

'Invasion!' said Mink. The door slammed.

In every yard on the street children brought out knives and forks and pokers and old stovepipes and can-openers.

It was an interesting fact that this fury and bustle occurred only among the younger children. The older ones, those ten years and more, disdained the affair and marched scornfully off on hikes or played a more dignified version of hide-and-seek on their own.

Meanwhile, parents came and went in chromium beetles. Repair men came to repair the vacuum elevators in houses, to fix fluttering television sets or hammer upon stubborn food-delivery tubes. The adult civilization passed and repassed the busy youngsters, jealous of the fierce energy of the wild tots, tolerantly amused at their flourishings, longing to join in themselves.

'This and this and *this*,' said Mink, instructing the others with their assorted spoons and wrenches. 'Do that, and bring *that* over here. No! *Here*, ninny! Right. Now, get back while I fix this.' Tongue in teeth, face wrinkled in thought. 'Like that. See?'

'Yayyy!' shouted the kids.

Twelve-year-old Joseph Connors ran up.

'Go away,' said Mink straight at him.

'I wanna play,' said Joseph.

'Can't!' said Mink.

'Why not?'

'You'd just make fun of us.'

'Honest, I wouldn't.'

'No. We know *you*. Go away or we'll kick you.'

Another twelve-year-old boy whirred by on little motor skates. 'Hey, Joe!' Come on! Let them sissies play!'

Joseph showed reluctance and a certain wistfulness, 'I *want* to play.' he said.

'You're old,' said Mink firmly.

'Not *that* old,' said Joe sensibly.

'You'd only laugh and spoil the Invasion.'

The boy on the motor skates made a rude lip noise. 'Come on, Joe! Them and their fairies! Nuts!'

Joseph walked off slowly. He kept looking back, all down the block.

Mink was already busy again. She made a kind of apparatus with her gathered equipment. She had appointed another little girl with a pad and pencil to take down notes in painful slow scribbles. Their voices rose and fell in the warm sunlight.

All around them the city hummed. The streets were lined with good green and peaceful trees. Only the wind made a conflict across the city, across the country, across the continent. In a thousand other cities there were trees and children and avenues, business men in their quiet offices taping their voices or watching televisors. Rockets hovered like darning needles in the blue sky. There was the universal, quiet conceit and easiness of men accustomed to peace, quite certain there would never be trouble again. Arm in arm, men all over earth were a united front. The perfect weapons were held in equal trust by all nations. A situation of incredibly beautiful balance had been brought about. There were no traitors among men, no unhappy ones, no disgruntled ones; therefore the world was based upon a stable ground. Sunlight illumined half the world and the trees drowsed in a tide of warm air.

Mink's mother, from her upstairs window, gazed down.

The children. She looked upon them and shook her head. Well, they'd eat well, sleep well, and be in school on Monday. Bless their vigorous little bodies. She listened.

Mink talked earnestly to someone near the rose bush— though there was no one there.

These odd children. And the little girl, what was her name? Anna? Anna took notes on a pad. First, Mink asked the rose bush a question, then called the answer to Anna.

'Triangle,' said Mink.

'What's a tri,' said Anna with difficulty, 'angle?'

'Never mind,' said Mink.

'How you spell it?' asked Anna.

'T-r-i——' spelled Mink slowly, then snapped, 'Oh, spell it yourself!' She went on to other words. 'Beam,' she said.

'I haven't got tri,' said Anna, 'angle down yet!'

'Well, hurry, hurry!' cried Mink.

Mink's mother leaned out of the upstairs window. 'A-n-g-l-e,' she spelled down at Anna.

'Oh, thanks, Mrs. Morris,' said Anna.

'Certainly,' said Mink's mother and withdrew, laughing, to dust the hall with an electro-duster magnet.

The voices wavered on the shimmery air. 'Beam,' said Anna. Fading.

'Four-nine-seven-A-and-B-and-X,' said Mink, far away, seriously. 'And a fork and a string and a—hex-hex-agony—hexagon*al*!'

At lunch Mink gulped milk at one toss and was at the door. Her mother slapped the table.

'You sit right back down,' commanded Mrs. Morris. 'Hot soup in a minute.' She poked a red button on the kitchen butler, and ten seconds later something landed with a bump in the rubber receiver. Mrs. Morris opened it, took out a can with a pair of aluminium holders, unsealed it with a flick, and poured hot soup into a bowl.

During all this Mink fidgeted. 'Hurry, Mom! This is a matter of life and death! Aw——'

'I was the same way at your age. Always life and death. I know.'

Mink banged away at the soup.

'Slow down,' said Mom.

'Can't,' said Mink. 'Drill's waiting for me.'

'Who's Drill? What a peculiar name,' said Mom.

'You don't know him,' said Mink.

'A new boy in the neighbourhood?' asked Mom.

'He's new all right,' said Mink. She started on her second bowl.

'Which one is Drill?' asked Mom.

'He's around,' said Mink evasively. 'You'll make fun. Everybody pokes fun. Gee, darn.'

'Is Drill shy?'

'Yes. No. In a way. Gosh, Mom, I got to run if we want to have the Invasion!'

'Who's invading what?'

'Martians invading Earth. Well, not exactly Martians. They're—I don't know. From up.' She pointed with her spoon.

'And *inside*,' said Mom, touching Mink's feverish brow.

Mink rebelled. 'You're laughing! You'd kill Drill and everybody.'

'I didn't mean to,' said Mom. 'Drill's a Martian?'

'No. He's—well—maybe from Jupiter or Saturn or Venus. Anyway, he's had a hard time.'

'I imagine.' Mrs. Morris hid her mouth behind her hand. 'They couldn't figure a way to attack Earth.'

'We're impregnable,' said Mom in mock seriousness.

'That's the word Drill used! Impreg —— That was the word, Mom.'

'My, my, Drill's a brilliant little boy. Two-bit words.'

'They couldn't figure a way to attack, Mom. Drill says— he says in order to make a good fight you got to have a new way of surprising people. That way you win. And he says also you got to have help from your enemy.'

'A fifth column,' said Mom.

'Yeah. That's what Drill said. And they couldn't figure a way to surprise Earth or get help.'

'No wonder. We're pretty darn strong.' Mom laughed, cleaning up. Mink sat there, staring at the table, seeing what she was talking about.

'Until, one day,' whispered Mink melodramatically, 'they thought of children!'

'*Well!*' said Mrs. Morris brightly.

'And they thought of how grown-ups are so busy they never look under rose bushes or on lawns!'

'Only for snails and fungus.'

'And then there's something about dim-dims.'

'Dim-dims?'

'Dimens-shuns.'

'Dimensions?'

'Four of 'em! And there's something about kids under nine and imagination. It's real funny to hear Drill talk.'

II

Mrs, Morris was tired. 'Well, it must be funny. You're keeping Drill waiting now. It's getting late in the day and, if you want to have your Invasion before your supper bath, you'd better jump.'

'Do I have to take a bath?' growled Mink.

'You do! Why is it children hate water? No matter what age you live in children hate water behind the ears!'

'Drill says I won't have to take baths,' said Mink.

'Oh, he does, does he?'

'He told all the kids that. No more baths. And we can stay up till ten o'clock and go to two televisor shows on Saturday 'stead of one!'

'Well, Mr. Drill better mind his p's and q's. I'll call up his mother and——'

Mink went to the door. 'We're having trouble with guys like Pete Britz and Dale Jerrick. They're growing up. They make fun. They're worse than parents. They just won't believe in Drill. They're so snooty, 'cause they're growing up. You'd think they'd know better. They were little only a coupla years ago. I hate them worst. We'll kill them *first*.'

'Your father and me last?'

'Drill says you're dangerous. Know why? 'Cause you don't believe in Martians! They're going to let *us* run the world. Well, not just us, but the kids over in the next block, too. I might be queen.' She opened the door.

'Mom?'

'Yes?'

'What's lodge-ick?'

'Logic? Why, dear, logic is knowing what things are true and not true.'

'He *mentioned* that,' said Mink. 'And what's im-pres-sion-able?' It took her a minute to say it.

'Why, it means——' Her mother looked at the floor, laughing gently. 'It means—to be a child, dear.'

'Thanks for lunch!' Mink ran out, then stuck her head back in. 'Mom, I'll be sure you won't be hurt much, really!'

'Well, thanks,' said Mom.

Slam went the door.

At four o'clock the audio-visor buzzed. Mrs. Morris flipped the tab. 'Hello, Helen!' she said in welcome.

'Hello, Mary. How are things in New York?'

'Fine. How are things in Scranton? You look tired.'

'So do you. The children. Underfoot,' said Helen.

Mrs. Morris sighed. 'My Mink too. The super-invasion.'

Helen laughed. 'Are your kids playing that game, too?'

'Lord, yes. Tomorrow it'll be geometrical jacks and motorized hopscotch. Were we this bad when we were kids in '48?'

'Worse. Japs and Nazis. Don't know how my parents put up with me. Tomboy.'

'Parents learn to shut their ears.'

A silence.

'What's wrong, Mary?' asked Helen.

Mrs. Morris's eyes were half closed; her tongue slid slowly, thoughtfully, over her lower lip. 'Eh?' She jerked. 'Oh, nothing. Just thought about *that*. Shutting ears and such. Never mind. Where were we?'

'My boy Tim's got a crush on some guy named—*Drill*, I think it was.'

'Must be a new password. Mink likes him too.'

'Didn't know it had got as far as New York. Word of mouth, I imagine. Looks like a scrap drive. I talked to Josephine and she said her kids—that's in Boston—are wild on this new game. It's sweeping the country.'

At this moment Mink trotted into the kitchen to gulp a glass of water. Mrs. Morris turned. 'How're things going?'

'Almost finished,' said Mink.

'Swell,' said Mrs. Morris. 'What's *that*?'

'A yo-yo,' said Mink. 'Watch.'

She flung the yo-yo down its string. Reaching the end it——

It vanished.

'See?' said Mink. 'Ope!' Dibbling her finger, she made the yo-yo reappear and zip up the string.

'Do that again,' said her mother.

'Can't. Zero hour's five o'clock. 'Bye!' Mink exited, zipping her yo-yo.

On the audio-visor, Helen laughed. 'Tim brought one of those yo-yos in this morning, but when I got curious he said he wouldn't show it to me, and when I tried to work it, finally, it wouldn't work.'

'You're not *impressionable*,' said Mrs. Morris.

'What?'

'Never mind. Something I thought of. Can I help you, Helen?'

'I wanted to get that black-and-white cake recipe——'

The hour drowsed by. The day waned. The sun lowered in the peaceful blue sky. Shadows lengthened on the green lawns. The laughter and excitement continued. One little girl ran away, crying. Mrs. Morris came out the front door.

'Mink, was that Peggy Ann crying?'

Mink was bent over in the yard, near the rose bush. 'Yeah. She's a scarebaby. We won't let her play, now. She's getting too old to play. I guess she grew up all of a sudden.'

'Is that why she cried? Nonsense. Give me a civil answer, young lady, or inside you come!'

Mink whirled in consternation, mixed with irritation. 'I can't quit now. It's almost time. I'll be good. I'm sorry.'

'Did you hit Peggy Ann?'

'No, honest. You ask her. It was something—well, she's just a scaredy pants.'

The ring of children drew in around Mink where she scowled at her work with spoons and a kind of square-shaped arrangement of hammers and pipes. 'There and there,' murmured Mink.

'What's wrong?' said Mrs. Morris.

'Drill's stuck. Half-way. If we could only get him all the way through it'd be easier. Then all the others could come through after him.'

'Can I help?'

'No'm, thanks. I'll fix it.'

'All right. I'll call you for your bath in half an hour. I'm tired of watching you.'

She went in and sat in the electric relaxing chair, sipping a little beer from a half-empty glass. The chair massaged her back. Children, children. Children and love and hate, side by side. Sometimes children loved you, hated you—all in half a second. Strange children, did they ever forget or forgive the whippings and the harsh, strict words of command? She wondered. How can you ever forget or forgive those over and above you, those tall and silly dictators?

Time passed. A curious, waiting silence came upon the street, deepening.

Five o'clock. A clock sang softly somewhere in the house in a quiet musical voice: 'Five o'clock—five o'clock. Time's a-wasting. Five o'clock,' and purred away into silence.

Zero hour.

Mrs. Morris chuckled in her throat. Zero hour.

A beetle car hummed into the driveway. Mr. Morris. Mrs. Morris smiled. Mr. Morris got out of the beetle, locked it, and called hello to Mink at her work. Mink ignored him. He laughed and stood for a moment watching the children. Then he walked up the front steps.

'Hello, darling.'

'Hello, Henry.'

She strained forward on the edge of the chair, listening. The children were silent. Too silent.

He emptied his pipe, refilled it. 'Swell day. Makes you glad to be alive.'

Buzz.

'What's that?' asked Henry.

'I don't know.' She got up suddenly, her eyes widening. She was going to say something. She stopped it. Ridiculous. Her nerves jumped. 'Those children haven't anything dangerous out there, have they?' she said.

'Nothing but pipes and hammers. Why?'

'Nothing electrical?'

'Heck, no,' said Henry. 'I looked.'

She walked to the kitchen. The buzzing continued. 'Just the same, you'd better go tell them to quit. It's after five. Tell them——' Her eyes widened and narrowed. 'Tell them to put off their Invasion until tomorrow.' She laughed, nervously.

The buzzing grew louder.

'What are they up to? I'd better go look, all right.'

The explosion!

The house shook with dull sound. There were other explosions in other yards on the streets.

Involuntarily, Mrs. Morris screamed. 'Up this way!' she cried senselessly, knowing no sense, no reason. Perhaps she saw something from the corners of her eyes; perhaps she smelled a new odour or heard a new noise. There was no time to argue with Henry to convince him. Let him think her insane. Yes, insane! Shrieking, she ran upstairs. He ran after her to see what she was up to. 'In the attic!' she screamed. 'That's where it is!' It was only a poor excuse to get him in the attic in time. Oh, God—in time!

Another explosion outside. The children screamed with delight, as if at a great fireworks display.

'It's not in the attic!' cried Henry. 'It's outside!'

'No, no!' Wheezing, gasping, she fumbled at the attic door. 'I'll show you. Hurry! I'll show you!'

They tumbled into the attic. She slammed the door, locked it, took the key, threw it into a far cluttered corner.

She was babbling wild stuff now. It came out of her. All the subconscious suspicion and fear that had gathered secretly all afternoon and fermented like a wine in her. All the little revelations and knowledges and sense that had bothered her all day and which she had, logically and carefully and sensibly, rejected and censored. Now it exploded in her and shook her to bits.

'There, there,' she said, sobbing against the door. 'We're safe until tonight. Maybe we can sneak out. Maybe we can escape!'

Henry blew up too, but for another reason. 'Are you crazy? Why'd you throw that key away? Damn it, honey!'

'Yes, yes, I'm crazy, if it helps, but stay here with me!'

'I don't know how in hell I *can* get out!'

'Quiet. They'll hear us. Oh, God, they'll find us soon enough——'

Below them, Mink's voice. The husband stopped. There was a great universal humming and sizzling, a screaming and giggling. Downstairs the audio-televisor buzzed and buzzed insistently, alarmingly, violently. *Is that Helen calling?* thought Mrs. Morris. *And is she calling about what I think she's calling about?*

Footsteps came into the house. Heavy footsteps.

'Who's coming in my house?' demanded Henry angrily. 'Who's tramping around down there?'

Heavy feet. Twenty, thirty, forty, fifty of them. Fifty persons crowding into the house. The humming. The giggling of the children. 'This way!' cried Mink, below.

'Who's downstairs?' roared Henry. 'Who's there?'

'Hush. Oh, nononononono!' said his wife weakly, holding him. 'Please, be quiet. They might go away.'

'Mom?' called Mink. 'Dad?' A pause. 'Where are you?'

Heavy footsteps, heavy, heavy, very *heavy* footsteps, came up the stairs. Mink leading them.

'Mum?' A hesitation. 'Dad?' A waiting, a silence.

Humming. Footsteps towards the attic. Mink's first.

They trembled together in silence in the attic, Mr. and Mrs. Morris. For some reason the electric humming, the queer cold light suddenly visible under the door crack, the strange odour and the alien sound of eagerness in Mink's voice finally got through to Henry Morris too. He stood, shivering, in the dark silence, his wife beside him.

'Mom! Dad!'

Footsteps. A little humming sound. The attic-lock melted. The door opened. Mink peered inside, tall blue shadows behind her.

'Peekaboo,' said Mink.

THE CRYSTAL EGG

H. G. WELLS

THERE WAS, until a year ago, a little and very grimy-looking shop near Seven Dials, over which, in weather-worn yellow lettering, the name of 'C. Cave, Naturalist and Dealer in Antiques,' was inscribed. The contents of its window were curiously variegated. They comprised some elephant tusks and an imperfect set of chessmen, beads and weapons, a box of eyes, two skulls of tigers and one human, several moth-eaten stuffed monkeys (one holding a lamp), an old-fashioned cabinet, a fly-blown ostrich egg, or so, some fishing-tackle, and an extraordinarily dirty, empty glass fish-tank. There was also, at the moment the story begins, a mass of crystal, worked into the shape of an egg and brilliantly polished. And at that two people who stood outside the window were looking, one of them a tall, thin clergyman, the other a black-bearded young man of dusky complexion and unobtrusive costume. The dusky man spoke with eager gesticulation, and seemed anxious for his companion to purchase the article.

While they were there, Mr. Cave came into his shop, his beard still wagging with the bread and butter of his tea. When he saw these men and the object of their regard, his countenance fell. He glanced guiltily over his shoulder, and softly shut the door. He was a little old man, with pale face and peculiar watery blue eyes; his hair was a dirty grey, and he wore a shabby blue frock-coat, an ancient silk hat, and carpet slippers very much down at heel. He remained watching the two men as they talked. The clergyman went deep into his trouser pocket, examined a handful of money, and showed his teeth in an agreeable smile. Mr. Cave seemed still more depressed when they came into the shop.

The clergyman, without any ceremony, asked the price of the crystal egg. Mr. Cave glanced nervously towards the door leading into the parlour, and said five pounds. The clergyman protested that the price was high, to his companion as well as to Mr. Cave—it was, indeed, very much more than Mr. Cave had intended to ask when he had stocked the article—and an attempt at bargaining ensued. Mr. Cave stepped to the shop door, and held it open. 'Five pounds is my price,' he said, as though he wished to save himself the trouble of unprofitable discussion. As he did so, the upper portion of a woman's face appeared above the blind in the glass upper panel of the door leading into the parlour, and stared curiously at the two customers. 'Five pounds is my price,' said Mr. Cave, with a quiver in his voice.

The swarthy young man had so far remained a spectator watching Cave keenly. Now he spoke. 'Give him five pounds,' he said. The clergyman glanced at him to see if he were in earnest, and when he looked at Mr. Cave again, he saw that the latter's face was white. 'It's a lot of money,' said the clergyman, and diving into his pocket, began counting his resources. He had little more than thirty shillings, and he appealed to his companion, with whom he seemed to be on terms of considerable intimacy. This gave Mr. Cave an opportunity of collecting his thoughts, and he began to explain in an agitated manner that the crystal was not, as a matter of fact, entirely free for sale. His two customers were naturally surprised at this, and inquired why he had not thought of that before he began to bargain. Mr. Cave became confused, but he stuck to his story, that the crystal was not in the market that afternoon, that a probable purchaser of it had already appeared. The two, treating this as an attempt to raise the price still further, made as if they would leave the shop. But at this point the parlour door opened and the owner of the dark fringe and the little eyes appeared.

She was a coarse-featured, corpulent woman, younger and very much larger than Mr. Cave; she walked heavily, and her face was flushed. 'That crystal *is* for sale,' she said. 'And five pounds is a good enough price for it. I can't think what you're about, Cave, not to take the gentleman's offer!'

Mr. Cave greatly perturbed by the interruption, looked angrily at her over the rims of his spectacles, and without excessive assurance, asserted his right to manage his business in his own way. An altercation began. The two customers watched the scene with interest and some amusement, occasionally assisting Mrs. Cave with suggestions. Mr. Cave, hard driven, persisted in a confused and impossible story of an inquiry for the crystal that morning, and his agitation became painful. But he stuck to his point with extraordinary persistence. It was the young Oriental who ended this curious controversy. He proposed that they should call again in the course of two days—so as to give the alleged inquirer a fair chance. 'And then we must insist,' said the clergyman. 'Five pounds.' Mrs. Cave took it on herself to apologize for her husband, explaining that he was sometimes 'a little odd,' and as the two customers left, the couple prepared for a free discussion of the incident in all its bearings.

Mrs. Cave talked to her husband with singular directness. The poor little man, quivering with emotion, muddled himself between his stories, maintaining on the one hand that he had another customer in view, and on the other asserting that the crystal was honestly worth ten guineas. 'Why did you ask five pounds?' said his wife. '*Do* let me manage my business my own way!' said Mr. Cave.

Mr. Cave had living with him a stepdaughter and a

stepson, and at supper that night the transaction was re-discussed. None of them had a high opinion of Mr. Cave's business methods, and this action seemed a culminating folly.

'It's my opinion he's refused that crystal before,' said the stepson, a loose-limbed lout of eighteen.

'*But Five Pounds!*' said the stepdaughter, an argumentative young woman of six-and-twenty.

Mr. Cave's answers were wretched; he could only mumble weak assertions that he knew his own business best. They drove him from his half-eaten supper into the shop, to close it for the night, his ears aflame and tears of vexation behind his spectacles. Why had he left the crystal in the window so long? The folly of it! That was the trouble closest in his mind. For a time he could see no way of evading sale.

After supper his stepdaughter and stepson smartened themselves up and went out and his wife retired upstairs to reflect upon the business aspects of the crystal, over a little sugar and lemon and so forth in hot water. Mr. Cave went into the shop, and stayed there until late, ostensibly to make ornamental rockeries for gold-fish cases, but really for a private purpose that will be better explained later. The next day Mrs. Cave found that the crystal had been removed from the window, and was lying behind some second-hand books on angling. She replaced it in a conspicuous position. But she did not argue further about it, as a nervous headache disinclined her from debate. Mr. Cave was always disinclined. The day passed disagreeably. Mr. Cave was, if anything, more absent-minded than usual, and uncommonly irritable withal. In the afternoon, when his wife was taking her customary sleep, he removed the crystal from the window again.

The next day Mr. Cave had to deliver a consignment of dog-fish at one of the hospital schools, where they were needed for dissection. In his absence Mrs. Cave's mind reverted to the topic of the crystal, and the methods of expenditure suitable to a windfall of five pounds. She had already devised some very agreeable expedients, among others a dress of green silk for herself and a trip to Richmond, when a jangling of the front door bell summoned her into the shop. The customer was an examination coach who came to complain of the non-delivery of certain frogs asked for the previous day. Mrs. Cave did not approve of this particular branch of Mr. Cave's business, and the gentleman, who had called in a somewhat aggressive mood, retired after a brief exchange of words—entirely civil, so far as he was concerned. Mrs. Cave's eye then naturally turned to the window; for the sight of the crystal was an assurance of the five pounds and of her dreams. What was her surprise to find it gone!

She went to the place behind the locker on the counter where she had discovered it the day before. It was not there; and she immediately began an eager search about the shop.

When Mr. Cave returned from his business with the dogfish, about a quarter to two in the afternoon, he found the shop in some confusion, and his wife, extremely exasperated and on her knees behind the counter, routing among his taxidermic material. Her face came up hot and angry over the counter, as the jangling bell announced his return, and she forthwith accused him of 'hiding it'.

'Hid *what?*' asked Mr. Cave.

'The crystal!'

At that Mr. Cave, apparently much surprised, rushed to the window. 'Isn't it there!' he said. 'Great Heavens! what has become of it?'

Just then Mr. Cave's stepson re-entered the shop from the inner room—he had come home a minute or so before Mr. Cave—and he was blaspheming freely. He was apprenticed to a second-hand furniture dealer down the road, but he had his meals at home, and he was naturally annoyed to find no dinner ready.

But when he heard of the loss of the crystal, he forgot

his meal, and his anger was diverted from his mother to his stepfather. Their first idea, of course, was that he had hidden it. But Mr. Cave stoutly denied all knowledge of its fate, freely offering his bedabbled affidavit in the matter— and at last worked up to the point of accusing, first his wife and then his stepson of having taken it with a view to a private sale. So began an exceedingly acrimonious and emotional discussion, which ended for Mrs. Cave in a peculiar nervous condition midway between hysterics and amuck, and caused the stepson to be half an hour late at the furniture establishment in the afternoon. Mr. Cave took refuge from his wife's emotions in the shop.

In the evening the matter was resumed, with less passion and in a judicial spirit, under the presidency of the stepdaughter. The supper passed unhappily and culminated in a painful scene. Mr. Cave gave way at last to extreme exasperation, and went out banging the front door violently. The rest of the family, having discussed him with the freedom his absence warranted, hunted the house from garret to cellar, hoping to light upon the crystal.

The next day the two customers called again. They were received by Mrs. Cave almost in tears. It transpired that no one *could* imagine all that she had stood from Cave at various times in her married pilgrimage . . .

She also gave a garbled account of the disappearance. The clergyman and the Oriental laughed silently at one another, and said it was very extraordinary. As Mrs. Cave seemed disposed to give them the complete history of her life they made to leave the shop. Thereupon Mrs. Cave, still clinging to hope, asked for the clergyman's address, so that, if she could get anything out of Cave, she might communicate it. The address was duly given, but apparently was afterwards mislaid. Mrs. Cave can remember nothing about it.

In the evening of that day the Caves seem to have exhausted their emotions, and Mr. Cave, who had been out in the afternoon, supped in a gloomy isolation that contrasted pleasantly with the impassioned controversy of the previous days. For some time matters were very badly strained in the Cave household, but neither crystal nor customer reappeared.

Now, without mincing the matter, we must admit that Mr. Cave was a liar. He knew perfectly well where the crystal was. It was in the rooms of Mr. Jacoby Wace, Assistant Demonstrator at St. Catherine's Hospital, Westbourne Street. It stood on the sideboard partially covered by a black velvet cloth, and beside a decanter of American whisky. It is from Mr. Wace, indeed, that the particulars upon which this narrative is based were derived. Cave had taken off the thing to the hospital hidden in the dog-fish sack, and there had pressed the young investigator to keep it for him. Mr. Wace was a little dubious at first. His relationship to Cave was peculiar. He had a taste for singular characters, and he had more than once invited the old man to smoke and drink in his rooms, and to unfold his rather amusing views of life in general and of his wife in particular. Mr. Wace had encountered Mrs. Cave, too, on occasions when Mr. Cave was not at home to attend to him. He knew the constant interference to which Cave was subjected, and having weighed the story judicially, he decided to give the crystal a refuge. Mr. Cave promised to explain the reasons for his remarkable affection for the crystal more fully on a later occasion, but he spoke distinctly of seeing visions therein. He called on Mr. Wace the same evening.

He told a complicated story. The crystal he said had come into his possession with other oddments at the forced sale of another curiosity dealer's effects, and not knowing what its value might be, he had ticketed it at ten shillings. It had hung upon his hands at that price for some months, and he was thinking of 'reducing the figure,' when he made a singular discovery.

At that time his health was very bad—and it must be borne in mind that, throughout all this experience his

physical condition was one of ebb—and he was in considerable distress by reason of the negligence, the positive ill-
treatment even, he received from his wife and stepchildren.
His wife was vain, extravagant, unfeeling, and had a growing taste for private drinking; his stepdaughter was mean
and over-reaching; and his stepson had conceived a violent
dislike for him, and lost no chance of showing it. The re-
quirements of his business pressed heavily upon him, and
Mr. Wace does not think that he was altogether free from
occasional intemperance. He had begun life in a comfortable position, he was a man of fair education, and he suf-
fered, for weeks at a stretch, from melancholia and in-
somnia. Afraid to disturb his family, he would slip quietly
from his wife's side, when his thoughts became intolerable,
and wander about the house. And about three o'clock one
morning, late in August, chance directed him into the shop.

The dirty little place was impenetrably black except in
one spot, where he perceived an unusual glow of light.
Approaching this, he discovered it to be the crystal egg,
which was standing on the corner of the counter towards
the window. A thin ray smote through a crack in the
shutters, impinged upon the object, and seemed as it were
to fill its entire interior.

It occurred to Mr. Cave that this was not in accordance
with the laws of optics as he had known them in his
younger days. He could understand the rays being refracted
by the crystal and coming to a focus in its interior, but
this diffusion jarred with his physical conceptions. He approached the crystal nearly, peering into it and around it,
with a transient revival of the scientific curiosity that in
his youth had determined his choice of a calling. He was
surprised to find the light not steady, but writhing within
the substance of the egg, as though that object was a hollow sphere of some luminous vapour. In moving about to
get different points of view, he suddenly found that he had
come between it and the ray, and that the crystal none
the less remained luminous. Greatly astonished, he lifted

it out of the light ray and carried it to the darkest part of the shop. It remained bright for some four or five minutes, when it slowly faded and went out. He placed it in the thin streak of daylight, and its luminousness was almost immediately restored.

So far, at least, Mr. Wace was able to verify the remarkable story of Mr. Cave. He has himself repeatedly held this crystal in a ray of light (which had to be of a less diameter than one millimetre). And in a perfect darkness, such as could be produced by velvet wrapping, the crystal did undoubtedly appear very faintly phosphorescent. It would seem, however, that the luminousness was of some exceptional sort, and not equally visible to all eyes; for Mr. Harbinger—whose name will be familiar to the scientific reader in connection with the Pasteur Institute—was quite unable to see any light whatever. And Mr. Wace's own capacity for its appreciation was out of comparison inferior to that of Mr. Cave's. Even with Mr. Cave the power varied very considerably; his vision was most vivid during states of extreme weakness and fatigue.

Now, from the outset, this light in the crystal exercised a curious fascination upon Mr. Cave. And it says more for his loneliness of soul than a volume of pathetic writing could do, that he told no human being of his curious observations. He seems to have been living in such an atmosphere of petty spite that to admit the existence of a pleasure would have been to risk the loss of it. He found that as the dawn advanced, and the amount of diffused light increased, the crystal became to all appearance non-luminous. And for some time he was unable to see anything in it, except at night-time, in dark corners of the shop.

But the use of an old velvet cloth, which he used as a background for a collection of minerals, occurred to him, and by doubling this, and putting it over his head and hands, he was able to get a sight of the luminous movement within the crystal even in the day-time. He was very cautious lest he should be thus discovered by his wife, and

I

he practised this occupation only in the afternoons, while she was asleep upstairs, and then circumspectly in a hollow under the counter.

And one day, turning the crystal about in his hands, he saw something. It came and went like a flash, but it gave him the impression that the object had for a moment opened to him the view of a wide and spacious and strange country; and turning it about, he did, just as the light faded, see the same vision again.

Now it would be tedious and unnecessary to state all the phases of Mr. Cave's discovery from this point. Suffice that the effect was this: the crystal, being peered into at an angle of about 137 degrees from the direction of the illuminating ray, gave a clear and consistent picture of a wide and peculiar countryside. It was not dream-like at all: it produced a definite impression of reality, and the better the light the more real and solid it seemed. It was a moving picture: that is to say, certain objects moved in it, but slowly in an orderly manner like real things, and, according as the direction of the lighting and vision changed, the picture changed also. It must, indeed, have been like looking through an oval glass at a view, and turning the glass about to get at different aspects.

Mr. Cave's statements, Mr. Wace assures me, were extremely circumstantial, and entirely free from any of that emotional quality that taints hallucinatory impressions. But it must be remembered that all the efforts of Mr. Wace to see any similar clarity in the faint opalescence of the crystal were wholly unsuccessful, try as he would. The difference in intensity of the impressions received by the two men was very great, and it is quite conceivable that what was a view to Mr. Cave was a mere blurred nebulosity to Mr. Wace.

The view, as Mr. Cave described it, was invariably of an extensive plain, and he seemed always to be looking at it from a considerable height, as if from a tower or a mast. To the east and to the west the plain was bounded at a

remote distance by vast reddish cliffs, which reminded him
of those he had seen in some picture: but what the picture was Mr. Wace was unable to ascertain. These cliffs
passed north and south—he could tell the points of the
compass by the stars that were visible of a night—receding in an almost illimitable perspective and fading into the
mists of the distance before they met. He was nearer the
eastern set of cliffs; on the occasion of his first vision the
sun was rising over them, and black against the sunlight
and pale against their shadow appeared a multitude of
soaring forms that Mr. Cave regarded as birds. A vast
range of buildings spread below him; he seemed to be looking down upon them, and as they approached the blurred
and refracted edge of the picture they became indistinct.
There were also trees curious in shape, and in colouring a
deep mossy green and an exquisite grey, beside a wide and
shining canal. And something great and brilliantly coloured
flew across the picture. But the first time Mr. Cave saw
these pictures he saw only in flashes, his hands shook, his
head moved, the vision came and went, and grew foggy
and indistinct. And at first he had the greatest difficulty in
finding the picture again once the direction of it was lost.

His next clear vision, which came about a week after
the first, the interval having yielded nothing but tantalizing glimpses and some useful experience, showed him the
view down the length of the valley. The view was different,
but he had a curious persuasion, which his subsequent observations abundantly confirmed, that he was regarding the
strange world from exactly the same spot, although he was
looking in a different direction. The long façade of the
great building, whose roof he had looked down upon before, was now receding in perspective. He recognized the
roof. In the front of the façade was a terrace of massive
proportions and extraordinary length, and down the middle
of the terrace, at certain intervals, stood huge but very
graceful masts, bearing small shiny objects which reflected
the setting sun. The import of these small objects did not

occur to Mr. Cave until some time after, as he was describing the scene to Mr. Wace. The terrace overhung a
thicket of the most luxuriant and graceful vegetation, and
beyond this was a wide grassy lawn on which certain
broad creatures, in form like beetles but enormously larger,
reposed. Beyond this again was a richly decorated causeway of pinkish stone; and beyond that, and lined with
dense red weeds, and passing up the valley exactly parallel
with the distant cliffs, was a broad and mirror-like expanse
of water. The air seemed full of squadrons of great birds,
manœuvring in stately curves; and across the river was a
multitude of splendid buildings, richly coloured and glittering with metallic tracery and facets, among a forest of
moss-like and lichenous trees. And suddenly something
flapped repeatedly across the vision, like the fluttering of
a jewelled fan or the beating of a wing, and a face, or
rather the upper part of a face with very large eyes, came,
as it were, close to his own and as if on the other side of
the crystal. Mr. Cave was so startled and so impressed by
the absolute reality of these eyes that he drew his head
back from the crystal to look behind it. He had become so
absorbed in watching that he was quite surprised to find
himself in the cool darkness of his little shop, with its
familiar odour of methyl, mustiness, and decay. And as he
blinked about him, the glowing crystal faded and went out.

Such were the first general impressions of Mr. Cave. The
story is curiously direct and circumstantial. From the outset, when the valley first flashed momentarily on his senses,
his imagination was strangely affected, and as he began to
appreciate the details of the scene he saw, his wonder rose
to the point of a passion. He went about his business list-
less and distraught, thinking only of the time when he
should be able to return to his watching. And then a few
weeks after his first sight of the valley came the two customers, the stress and excitement of their offer, and the
narrow escape of the crystal from sale, as I have already
told.

Now, while the thing was Mr. Cave's secret, it remained a mere wonder, a thing to creep to covertly and peep at, as a child might peep upon a forbidden garden. But Mr. Wace has, for a young scientific investigator, a particularly lucid and consecutive habit of mind. Directly the crystal and its story came to him, and he had satisfied himself, by seeing the phosphorescence with his own eyes, that there really was a certain evidence for Mr. Cave's statements, he proceeded to develop the matter systematically. Mr. Cave was only too eager to come and feast his eyes on this wonderland he saw, and he came every night from half-past eight until half-past ten, and sometimes, in Mr. Wace's absence during the day. On Sunday afternoons, also, he came. From the outset Mr. Wace made copious notes, and it was due to his scientific method that the relation between the direction from which the initiating ray entered the crystal and the orientation of the picture were proved. And, by covering the crystal in a box perforated only with a small aperture to admit the exciting ray, and by substituting black holland for his buff blinds, he greatly improved the conditions of the observations; so that in a little while they were able to survey the valley in any direction they desired.

So having cleared the way, we may give a brief account of this visionary world within the crystal. The things were in all cases seen by Mr. Cave, and the method of working was invariably for him to watch the crystal and report what he saw, while Mr. Wace (who as a science student had learnt the trick of writing in the dark) wrote a brief note of his report. When the crystal faded, it was put into its box in the proper position and the electric light turned on. Mr. Wace asked questions, and suggested observations to clear up difficult points. Nothing, indeed, could have been less visionary and more matter-of-fact.

The attention of Mr. Cave had been speedily directed to the bird-like creatures he had seen so abundantly present in each of his earlier visions. His first impression was soon corrected, and he considered for a time that they might represent a diurnal species of bat. Then he thought, grotesquely enough, that they might be cherubs. Their heads were round and curiously human, and it was the eyes of one of them that had so startled him on his second observation. They had broad, silvery wings, not feathered, but glistening almost as brilliantly as new-killed fish and with the same subtle play of colour, and these wings were not built on the plan of bird-wing or bat, Mr. Wace learned, but supported by curved ribs radiating from the body. (A sort of butterfly wing with curved ribs seems best to express their appearance.) The body was small, but fitted with two bunches of prehensile organs, like long tentacles, immediately under the mouth. Incredible as it appeared to Mr. Wace, the persuasion at last became irresistible that it was these creatures which owned the great quasi-human buildings and the magnificent garden that made the broad valley so splendid. And Mr. Cave perceived that the buildings, with other peculiarities, had no doors, but that the great circular windows, which opened freely, gave the creatures egress and entrance. They would alight upon their tentacles, fold their wings to a smallness almost rodlike, and hop into the interior. But among them was a multitude of smaller-winged creatures, like great dragon-flies and moths and flying beetles, and across the greensward brilliantly-coloured gigantic ground-beetles crawled lazily to and fro. Moreover, on the causeways and terraces, large-headed creatures similar to the greater winged flies, but wingless, were visible, hopping busily upon their hand-like tangle of tentacles.

Allusion has already been made to the glittering objects upon masts that stood upon the terrace of the nearer building. It dawned upon Mr. Cave, after regarding one of these masts very fixedly on one particularly vivid day that the glittering object there was a crystal exactly like that into which he peered. And a still more careful scrutiny convinced him that each one in a vista of nearly twenty carried a similar object.

Occasionally one of the large flying creatures would flutter up to one, and folding its wings and coiling a number of its tentacles about the mast, would regard the crystal fixedly for a space—sometimes for as long as fifteen minutes. And a series of observations, made at the suggestion of Mr. Wace, convinced both watchers that, so far as this visionary world was concerned, the crystal into which they peered actually stood at the summit of the endmost mast on the terrace, and that on one occasion at least one of these inhabitants of this other world had looked into Mr. Cave's face while he was making these observations.

So much for the essential facts of this very singular story. Unless we dismiss it all as the ingenious fabrication of Mr. Wace, we have to believe one of two things: either that Mr. Cave's crystal was in two worlds at once, and that while it was carried about in one, it remained stationary in the other, which seems altogether absurd; or else that it had some peculiar relation of sympathy with another and exactly similar crystal in this other world, so that what was seen in the interior of the one in this world was, under suitable conditions, visible to an observer in the corresponding crystal in the other world; and *vice versa*. At present, indeed, we do not know of any way in which two crystals could so come *en rapport*, but nowadays we know enough to understand that the thing is not altogether impossible. This view of the crystals as *en rapport* was the supposition that occurred to Mr. Wace, and to me at least it seems extremely plausible. . . .

And where was this other world? On this, also, the alert intelligence of Mr. Wace speedily threw light. After sunset, the sky darkened rapidly—there was a very brief twilight interval indeed—and the stars shone out. They were recognizably the same as those we see, arranged in the same constellations. Mr. Cave recognized the Bear, the

Pleiades, Aldebaran, and Sirius; so that the other world must be somewhere in the solar system, and, at the utmost, only a few hundreds of millions of miles from our own. Following up this clue, Mr. Wace learned that the midnight sky was a darker blue even than our midwinter sky, and that the sun seemed a little smaller. *And there were two small moons!* 'like our moon but smaller, and quite differently marked,' one of which moved so rapidly that its motion was clearly visible, as one regarded it. These moons were never high in the sky, but vanished as they rose : that is, every time they revolved they were eclipsed because they were so near their primary planet. And all this answers quite completely, although Mr. Cave did not know it, to what must be the condition of things on Mars.

Indeed, it seems an exceedingly plausible conclusion that peering into this crystal Mr. Cave did actually see the planet Mars and its inhabitants. And if that be the case, then the evening star that shone so brilliantly in the sky of that distant vision was neither more nor less than our own familiar earth.

For a time the Martians—if they were Martians—do not seem to have known of Mr. Cave's inspection. Once or twice one would come to peer, and go away very shortly to some other mast, as though the vision was unsatisfactory. During this time Mr. Cave was able to watch the proceedings of these winged people without being disturbed by their attentions, and although his report is necessarily vague and fragmentary, it is nevertheless very suggestive. Imagine the impression of humanity a Martian observer would get who, after a difficult process of preparation and with considerable fatigue to the eyes, was able to peer at London from the steeple of St. Martin's Church for stretches, at longest, of four minutes at a time. Mr. Cave was unable to ascertain if the winged Martians were the same as the Martians who hopped about the causeways and terraces, and if the latter could put on wings at will. He several times saw certain clumsy bipeds, dimly suggestive of apes, white and partially translucent, feeding among certain of the lichenous trees, and once some of these fled before one of the hopping, round-headed Martians. The latter caught one in its tentacles, and then the picture faded suddenly and left Mr. Cave most tantalizingly in the dark. On another occasion a vast thing, that Mr Cave thought at first was some gigantic insect, appeared advancing along the causeway beside the canal with extraordinary rapidity. As this drew nearer Mr. Cave perceived that it was a mechanism of shining metals and of extraordinary complexity. And then, when he looked again, it had passed out of sight.

After a time Mr. Wace aspired to attract the attention of the Martians, and the next time that the strange eyes of one of them appeared close to the crystal Mr. Cave cried out and sprang away, and they immediately turned on the light and began to gesticulate in a manner suggestive of signalling. But when at last Mr. Cave examined the crystal again the Martian had departed.

Thus far these observations had progressed in early November, and then Mr. Cave, feeling that the suspicions of his family about the crystal were allayed, began to take it to and fro with him in order that, as occasion arose in the daytime or night, he might comfort himself with what was fast becoming the most real thing in his existence.

In December Mr. Wace's work in connection with a forthcoming examination became heavy, the sittings were reluctantly suspended for a week, and for ten or eleven days—he is not quite sure which— he saw nothing of Cave. He then grew anxious to resume these investigations, and, the stress of his seasonal labours being abated, he went down to Seven Dials. At the corner he noticed a shutter before a bird fancier's window and then another at a cobbler's. Mr. Cave's shop was closed.

He rapped and the door was opened by the stepson in black. He at once called Mrs. Cave, who was, Mr. Wace could not but observe, in cheap but ample widow's weeds of the most imposing pattern. Without any very great surprise Mr. Wace learnt that Cave was dead and already buried. She was in tears, and her voice was a little thick. She had just returned from Highgate. Her mind seemed occupied with her own prospects and the honourable details of the obsequies, but Mr. Wace was at last able to learn of the particulars of Cave's death. He had been found dead in his shop in the early morning, the day after his last visit to Mr. Wace, and the crystal had been clasped in his stone-cold hands. His face was smiling, said Mrs. Cave, and the velvet cloth from the minerals lay on the floor at his feet. He must have been dead five or six hours when he was found.

This came as a great shock to Wace, and he began to reproach himself bitterly for having neglected the plain symptoms of the old man's ill-health. But his chief thought was of the crystal. He approached that topic in a gingerly manner, because he knew Mrs. Cave's peculiarities. He was dumbfounded to learn that it was sold.

Mrs. Cave's first impulse, directly Cave's body had been taken upstairs, had been to write to the mad clergyman who had offered five pounds for the crystal, informing him of its recovery; but after a violent hunt, in which her daughter joined her, they were convinced of the loss of his address. As they were without the means required to mourn and bury Cave in the elaborate style the dignity of an old Seven Dials inhabitant demands, they had appealed to a friendly fellow-tradesman in Great Portland Street. He had very kindly taken over a portion of the stock at a valuation. The valuation was his own, and the crystal egg was included in one of the lots. Mr. Wace, after a few suitable condolences, a little offhandedly proffered perhaps, hurried at once to Great Portland Street. But there he learned that the crystal egg had already been sold to a tall, dark man in grey. And there the material facts in this curious, and to me at least very suggestive, story come abruptly to an end. The Great Portland Street dealer did not know who the tall dark man in grey was, nor had he observed him with sufficient attention to describe him minutely. He did not even know which way this person had gone after leaving the shop. For a time Mr. Wace remained in the shop, trying the dealer's patience with hopeless questions, venting his own exasperation. And at last realizing abruptly that the whole thing had passed out of his hands, had vanished like a vision of the night, he returned to his own rooms, a little astonished to find the notes he had made still tangible and visible upon his untidy table.

His annoyance and disappointment were naturally very great. He made a second call (equally ineffectual) upon the Great Portland Street dealer, and he resorted to advertisements in such periodicals as were likely to come into the hands of a *bric-à-brac* collector. He also wrote letters to *The Daily Chronicle* and *Nature*, but both those periodicals, suspecting a hoax, asked him to reconsider his action before they printed, and he was advised that such a strange story, unfortunately so bare of supporting evidence, might imperil his reputation as an investigator. Moreover, the calls of his proper work were urgent. So that after a month or so, save for an occasional reminder to certain dealers, he had reluctantly to abandon the quest for the crystal egg, and from that day to this it remains undiscovered. Occasionally, however, he tells me, and I can quite believe him, he has bursts of zeal, in which he abandons his more urgent occupation and resumes the search.

Whether or not it will remain lost for ever, with the material and origin of it, are things equally speculative at the present time. If the present purchaser is a collector, one would have expected the inquiries of Mr. Wace to have reached him through the dealers. He has been able to discover Mr. Cave's clergyman and 'Oriental'—no other than the Rev. James Parker and young Prince of Bosso-Kuni in Java. I am obliged to them for certain particulars. The object of the Prince was simply curiosity—and extravagance.

He was so eager to buy because Cave was so oddly reluctant to sell. It is just as possible that the buyer in the second instance was simply a casual purchaser, and not a collector at all, and the crystal egg, for all I know, may at the present moment be within a mile of me, decorating a drawing-room or serving as a paper-weight—its remarkable functions all unknown. Indeed, it is partly with the idea of such a possibility that I have thrown this narrative into a form that will give it a chance of being read by the ordinary consumer of fiction.

My own ideas in the matter are practically identical with those of Mr. Wace. I believe the crystal on the mast in Mars and the crystal egg of Mr. Cave's to be in some physical, but at present quite inexplicable, way *en rapport*, and we both believe further that the terrestrial crystal must have been—possibly at some remote date—sent hither from that planet, in order to give the Martians a near view of our affairs. Possibly the fellows to the crystals on the other masts are also on our globe. No theory of hallucination suffices for the facts.

DORMANT

A. E. VAN VOGT

OLD WAS the island. Even the thing that lay in the outer channel, exposed to the rude wash of the open sea, had never guessed, when it was alive a million years before, that here was a protuberance of primeval earth itself.

The island was roughly three miles long and, at its widest, half a mile across. It curved tensely around a blue lagoon and the thin shape of its rocky, foam-ridden arms and hands came down towards the toe of the island—like a gigantic man bending over, striving to touch his feet and not quite making it.

Through the channel made by that gap between the toes and the fingers came the sea.

The water resented the channel. With an endless patience it fought to break the wall of rock, and the tumult of the waters was a special sound, a blend of all that was raucous and unseemly in the eternal quarrel between resisting land and encroaching wave.

At the very hub of the screaming waters lay Iilah, dead now almost for ever, forgotten by time and the universe.

Early in 1941 Japanese ships came and ran the gauntlet of dangerous waters into the quiet lagoon. From the deck of one of the ships a pair of curious eyes pondered the thing, where it lay in the path of the rushing sea. But the owner of those eyes was the servant of a government that frowned on extra-military ventures on the part of its personnel. And so the engineer Taku Onilo merely noted in his report that, 'At the mouth of this channel there lies a solid shape of glittery, rock-like substance about four hundred feet long and ninety feet wide.'

The little yellow men built their underground gas and oil tanks and departed towards the setting sun. The water rose and fell, rose and fell again. The days and the years drifted by, and the hand of time was heavy. The seasonal rains arrived on their rough schedule and washed away the marks of man. Green growth sprouted where machines had exposed the raw earth. The war ended. The underground tanks sagged a little in their beds of earth and cracks appeared in several main pipes. Slowly the oil drained off and for years a yellow-green oil slick brightened the gleam of the lagoon waters.

In the reaches of Bikini Atoll, hundreds of miles away, first one explosion, then another, started in motion an intricate pattern of radio-activated waters. The first seepage of that potent energy reached the island in the early autumn of 1946.

It was about two years later that a patient clerk, ransacking the records of the Imperial Japanese navy in Tokyo, reported the existence of the oil tanks. In due time —1950—the destroyer *Coulson* set forth on its routine voyage of examination.

The time of the nightmare was come.

Lieutenant Keith Maynard peered gloomily through his binoculars at the island. He was prepared to find something wrong, but he expected a distracting monotony of sameness, not something radically different. 'Usual undergrowth,' he muttered, 'and a backbone of semi-mountain running like a framework the length of the island, trees——' He stopped there.

A broad swath had been cut through the palms on the near shoreline. They were not just down. They were crushed deep into a furrow that was already alive with

grass and small growth. The furrow, which looked about a
hundred feet wide, led upwards from the beach to the side
of a hill, to where a large rock lay half-buried near the
top of the hill.

Puzzled, Maynard glanced down at the Japanese photo-
graphs of the island. Involuntarily, he turned towards his
executive officer, Lieutenant Gerson. 'Good lord!' he said.
'How did that rock get up *there*? It's not on any photo-
graphs.'

The moment he had spoken he regretted it. Gerson looked
at him, with his usual faint antagonism, shrugged and said,
'Maybe we've got the wrong island.'

Maynard did not answer that. He considered Gerson a
queer character. The man's tongue dripped ceaselessly with
irony.

'I'd say it weighs about two million tons. The Japs probably dragged it up there to confuse us.'

Maynard said nothing. He was annoyed that he had
made a comment. Particularly annoyed because, for a
moment, he had actually thought of the Japs in connection
with the rock. The weight estimate, which he instantly
recognized as probably fairly accurate, ended all his wilder
thoughts. If the Japs could move a rock weighing two
million tons they had also won the war. Still, it was very
curious and deserved investigation later.

They ran the channel without incident. It was wider
and deeper than Maynard had understood from the Jap
accounts, which made everything easy. Their midday meal
was eaten in the shelter of the lagoon. Maynard noted the
oil on the water and issued immediate warnings against
throwing matches overboard. After a brief talk with the
other officers, he decided that they would set fire to the
oil as soon as they had accomplished their mission and
were out of the lagoon.

About one-thirty, boats were lowered and they made
shore in quick order. In an hour, with the aid of tran-
scribed Japanese blueprints, they located the four buried

tanks. It took somewhat longer to assess the dimensions of the tanks and to discover that three of them were empty. Only the smallest, containing high-octane petrol, remained leakproof and still full. The value of that was about seventeen thousand dollars, not worth the attention of the larger navy tankers that were still cruising around, picking up odd lots of Japanese and American material. Maynard presumed that a lighter would eventually be dispatched for the petrol, but that was none of his business.

In spite of the speed with which his job had been accomplished, Maynard climbed wearily up to the deck just as darkness was falling. He must have overdone it a little because Gerson said too loudly, 'Worn out, sir?'

Maynard stiffened. And it was that comment, rather than any inclination, that decided him not to postpone his exploration of the rock. As soon as possible after the evening meal, he called for volunteers. It was pitch dark as the boat, with seven men and Bos'n's Mate Yewell and himself, was beached on the sands under the towering palms. The party headed inland.

There was no moon and the stars were scattered among remnant clouds of the rainy season just past. They walked in the furrow where the trees had been literally ploughed into the ground. In the pale light of the flashlights the spectacle of numerous trees, burned and planed into a smoothed levelness with the soil, was unnatural.

Maynard heard one of the men mumble. 'Must have been some freak of a typhoon did that.'

Not only a typhoon, Maynard decided, but a ravenous fire followed by a monstrous wind, so monstrous that—his thought paused. He couldn't imagine any storm big enough to lift a two-million-ton rock to the side of a hill a quarter of a mile long and four hundred feet above sea level. From nearby, the rock looked like nothing more than rough granite. In the beam of the flashlights it glinted with innumerable streaks of pink. Maynard led his party alongside it and the vastness of it grew upon him as he climbed past its four hundred feet of length and peered up at gleaming walls, like cliffs looming above him. The upper end, buried though it was deeper into the ground, rose at least fifty feet above his head.

The night had grown uncomfortably warm. Maynard was perspiring freely. He enjoyed a moment of weary pleasure in the thought that he was doing his duty under unpleasant circumstances. He stood uncertain, gloomily savouring the intense primitive silence of the night. 'Break off some samples here and there,' he said finally. 'Those pink streaks look interesting.'

It was a few seconds later that a man's scream of agony broke through the thrall of darkness.

Flashlights blinked on. They showed Seaman Hicks twisting on the ground beside the rock. In the bright flame of the lights the man's wrist showed as a smouldering, blackened husk with the entire hand completely burned off.

He had touched Iilah.

Maynard gave the desperately suffering man morphine and they rushed him back to the ship. Radio contact was established with base and a consulting surgeon gave cut by cut instructions on the operation. It was agreed that a hospital plane would be dispatched for the patient. There must have been some puzzlement at headquarters as to how the accident had occurred, because 'further information' was requested about the 'hot' rock. By morning the people at the other end were calling it a meteorite. Maynard, who did not normally question opinions offered by his superiors, frowned over the identification, and pointed out that this meteorite weighed two million tons and rested on the surface of the island.

'I'll send the assistant engineer officer to take its temperature,' he said.

An engine-room thermometer registered the rock's surface temperature at eight hundred-odd degrees Fahrenheit. The answer to that was a question that shocked Maynard.

K

'Why, yes,' he replied, 'we're getting mild radio-active reactions from the water, but nothing else. And nothing serious. Under the circumstances we'll withdraw from the lagoon at once and await the ships with the scientists.'

He ended that conversation, pale and shaken. Nine men, including himself, had walked along within a few yards of the rock, well within the deadly danger zone. In fact, even the *Coulson*, more than half a mile away, would have been affected.

But the gold leaves of the electroscope stood out stiff and the Geiger-Mueller counter clucked only when placed in the water and then only at long intervals. Relieved, Maynard went down to have another look at Seaman Hicks. The injured man slept uneasily but he was not dead, which was a good sign. When the hospital plane arrived there was a doctor aboard, who attended Hicks and then gave everyone on the destroyer a blood-count test. He came up on deck, a cheerful young man, and reported to Maynard.

'Well, it can't be what they suspect,' he said. 'Everybody's O.K., even Hicks, except for his hand. That burned awfully quick, if you ask me, for a temperature of only eight hundred.'

'I think his hand stuck,' said Maynard. And he shuddered. In his self-destructive fashion, he had mentally experienced the entire accident.

'So that's the rock,' said Dr. Clason. 'Does seem odd how it got there.'

They were still standing there five minutes later when a hideous screaming from below deck made a discordant sound on the still air of that remote island lagoon.

Something stirred in the depths of Iilah's awareness of himself, something that he had intended to do. He couldn't remember what.

That was the first real thought he had in late 1946, when he felt the impact of outside energy. And stirred with returning life. The outside flow waxed and waned. It was abnormally, abysmally dim. The crust of the planet that he knew had palpitated with the ebbing but potent energies of a world not yet cooled from its sun state. It was only slowly that Iilah realized the extent of the disaster that was his environment. At first he was inwardly inclined, too pallidly alive to be interested in externals.

He forced himself to become more conscious of his environment. He looked forth with his radar vision out upon a strange world. He was lying on a shallow plateau near the top of a mountain. The scene was desolate beyond his memory. There was not a glint nor pressure of atomic fire —not a bubble of boiling rock nor a swirl of energy heaved skyward by some vast interior explosion.

He did not think of what he saw as an island surrounded by an apparently limitless ocean. He saw the land below the water as well as above it. His vision, based as it was on ultra-ultra short waves, could not see water. He recognized that he was on an old and dying planet, where life had long since become extinct. Alone and dying on a forgotten planet—if he could only find the source of the energy that had revived him.

By a process of simple logic he started down the mountain in the direction from which the current of atomic energy seemed to be coming. Somehow, he found himself below it and had to levitate himself heavily back up. Once started upwards, he headed for the nearest peak, with the intention of seeing what was on the other side.

As he propelled himself out of the invisible, unsensed waters of the lagoon, two diametrically opposite phenomena affected him. He lost all contact with the waterborne current of atomic energy. And, simultaneously, the water ceased to inhibit the neutron and deuteron activity of his body. His life took on an increased intensity. The tendency to slow stiflement ended. His great form became a self-sustaining pile, capable of surviving for the normal radio-active lifespan of the elements that composed it—still on an immensely less than normal activity level for him.

Again, Iilah thought, 'There was something I was going to do.'

There was an increased flow of electrons through a score of gigantic cells as he strained to remember. It slowed gradually when no memory came. The fractional increase of his life energy brought with it a wider, more exact understanding of his situation. Wave on wave of perceptive radaric forces flowed from him to the Moon, to Mars, to all the planets of the Solar System—and the echoes that came back were examined with an alarmed awareness that out there, too, were dead bodies.

He was caught in the confines of a dead system, prisoned until the relentless exhaustion of his material structure brought him once more to *rapport* with the barren mass of the planet on which he was marooned. He realized now that he had been dead. Just how it happened he could not recall, except that explosively violent, frustrating substance had belched around him, buried him, and snuffed out his life processes. The atomic chemistry involved must eventually have converted the stuff into a harmless form, no longer capable of hindering him. But he was dead by then.

Now he was alive again, but in so dim a fashion that there was nothing to do but wait for the end. He waited.

In 1950 he watched the destroyer float towards him through the sky. Long before it slowed and stopped just below him, he had discovered that it was not a life-form related to him. It manufactured a dull internal heat and, through its exterior walls, he could see the vague glow of fires.

All that first day, Iilah waited for the creature to show awareness of him. But not a wave of life emanated from it. And yet it floated in the sky above the plateau, an impossible phenomenon, outside all his experience. To Iilah, who had no means of sensing water, who could not even imagine air, and whose ultra waves passed through human beings as if they did not exist, the reaction could mean only one thing—here was an alien life-form that had adapted itself to the dead world around him.

Gradually, Iilah grew excited. The thing could move freely above the surface of the planet. It would know if any source of atomic energy remained anywhere. The problem was to get into communication with it. The sun was high on the meridian of another day when Iilah directed the first questioning pattern of thought towards the destroyer. He aimed straight at the vaguely glowing fires in the engine room, where, he reasoned, would be the intelligence of the alien creature.

The thirty-four men who died in the spaces in and around the engine room and the fire room were buried on the shore. Their surviving comrades expected to stay there until the abandoned *Coulson* ceased to give off dangerous radio-active energies. On the seventh day, when transport planes were already dumping scientific equipment and personnel, three of the men fell sick and their blood count showed a fateful decrease in the number of red corpuscles. Although no orders had arrived, Maynard took alarm and ordered the entire crew shipped for observation to Hawaii.

He allowed the officers to make their own choice, but advised the second engineer officer, the first gunnery officer and several ensigns who had helped hoist the dead men up to the deck, to take no chances, but to grab space on the first planes. Although all were ordered to leave, several crew members asked permission to remain. And, after a careful questioning by Gerson, a dozen men who could prove that they had not been near the affected area were finally allowed to stay.

Maynard would have preferred to see Gerson himself depart, but in this he was disappointed. Of the officers who had been aboard the destroyer at the time of the disaster, Lieutenants Gerson, Lausson, and Haury, the latter two being gunnery officers, and Ensigns McPelty, Roberts, and Manchioff, remained on the beach.

Among the higher ratings remaining behind were the

chief commissary steward, Jenkins, and chief bos'n's mate, Yewell.

The navy group was ignored except that several times requests were made that they move their tents out of the way. Finally, when it seemed evident that they would be crowded out once more, Maynard, in annoyance, ordered the canvas moved well down the coast, where the palms opened up to form a grassy meadow.

Maynard grew puzzled, then grim, as the weeks passed and no orders arrived concerning the disposal of his command. In one of the Stateside papers that began to follow the scientists, the bulldozers, and cement mixers on to the island he read an item in an 'inside' column that gave him his first inkling. According to the columnist, there had been a squabble between navy bigwigs and the civilian members of the Atomic Energy Commission over control of the investigation. With the result that the navy had been ordered to 'stay out'.

Maynard read the account with mixed feelings and a dawning understanding that he was *the* navy representative on the island. The realization included a thrilling mental visualization of himself rising to the rank of admiral—if he handled the situation right. Just what would be right, aside from keeping a sharp eye on everything, he couldn't decide. It was an especially exquisite form of self-torture.

He couldn't sleep. He spent his days wandering as unobtrusively as possible through the ever vaster encampment of the army of scientists and their assistants. At night he had several hiding places from which he watched the brilliantly lighted beach.

It was a fabulous oasis of brightness in the dark vaulting vastness of a Pacific night. For a full mile, string upon string of lights spread along the whispering waters. They silhouetted and spotlighted the long, thick, back-curving, cement-like walls that reared up eerily, starting at the rim of the hill. Protective walls that were already soaring up around the rock itself, striving to block it off from all out-

side contact. Always, at midnight, the bulldozers ceased
their roarings, the cement-mixing trucks dumped their last
loads and scurried down the makeshift beach road to
silence. The already intricate organization settled into an
uneasy slumber. Maynard usually waited with the painful
patience of a man doing more than his duty. About one
o'clock, he too would make his way to bed.

The secret habit paid off. He was the only man who
actually witnessed the rock climb to the top of the hill.

It was a stupendous event. The time was about a quarter
to one and Maynard was on the point of calling it a day
when he heard the sound. It was like a truck emptying a
load of gravel. For a bare moment he thought of it entirely
in relation to his hiding place. His night-spying activities
were going to be found out. An instant after that the rock
reared up into the brilliance of the lights.

There was a roaring now of cement barriers crumbling
before that irresistible movement. Fifty, sixty, then ninety
feet of monster rock loomed up above the hill, slid with a
heavy power over the crown, and stopped.

For two months Iilah had watched the freighters breast
the channel. Just why they followed that route interested
him. And he wondered if there was some limitation on
them that kept them at such an exact level. What was
more interesting by far, however, was that in every case
the aliens would slide around the island, and disappear
behind a high promontory that was the beginning of the
east shore. In every case, after they had been gone for a
few days, they would slide into view again, glide through
the channel, and gradually move off through the sky.

During those months, Iilah caught tantalizing glimpses
of small, but much faster, winged ships that shot down
from a great height and disappeared behind the crest of
the hill to the east. Always to the east. His curiosity grew
enormous, but he was reluctant to waste energy. He grew
aware finally of a night-time haze of lights that brightened
the eastern sky at night. He set off the more violent ex-

plosions on his lower surface which made directive motion possible, and climbed the last seventy or so feet to the top of the hill. He regretted it immediately.

One ship lay a short distance offshore. The haze of lights along the eastern slope seemed to have no source. As he watched, scores of trucks and bulldozers raced around, some of them coming quite close to him. Just what they wanted, or what they were doing he could not make out. He sent several questioning thought-waves at various of the objects, but there was no response.

He gave it up as a bad job.

The rock was still resting on the top of the hill the next morning, poised so that both sides of the island were threatened by the stray bursts of energy which it gave off so erratically. Maynard heard his first account of the damage done from Jenkins, the chief commissary steward. Seven truck drivers and two bulldozer men dead, a dozen men suffering from glancing burns—and two months' labour wrecked.

There must have been a conference among the scientists, for shortly after noon, trucks and bulldozers, loaded with equipment, began to stream past the navy camp. A seaman, dispatched to follow them, reported that they were setting up camp on the point at the lower end of the island.

Just before dark a notable event took place. The director of the Project together with four executive scientists walked into the lighted area and asked for Maynard. The group was smiling and friendly. There was handshaking all around. Maynard introduced Gerson who, unfortunately, as far as Maynard was concerned, was in the camp at the moment. And then the visiting delegation got down to business.

'As you know,' said the director, 'the *Coulson* is only partially radio-active. The rear gun turret is quite unaffected, and we accordingly request that you co-operate with us and fire on the rock until it is broken into sections.'

It took Maynard a moment to recover from his astonishment, and to know what he would answer to that. At no time, during the next few days, did he question the belief of the scientists that the rock should be broken up and so rendered harmless. He refused their request and then doggedly continued to refuse it. It was not until the third day that he thought of a reason.

'Your precautions, gentlemen,' he said, 'are not sufficient. I do not consider that moving the camp out to the point is safeguard enough in the event that the rock should blow up. Now, of course, if I should receive a command from a naval authority to do as you wish . . .'

He left that sentence dangling, and saw from their disappointed faces that there must have been a feverish exchange of radio messages with their own headquarters. The arrival of a Kwajalein paper on the fourth day quoted a 'high' Washington naval officer as saying that 'any such decisions must be left to the judgment of the naval commander on the island.' It was also stated that, if a properly channelled request was made, the navy would be glad to send an atomic expert of its own to the scene.

It was obvious to Maynard that he was handling the situation exactly as his superiors desired. The only thing was that, even as he finished reading the account, the silence was broken by the unmistakable bark of a destroyer's five-inch guns, the sharpest of all gunfire sounds.

Unsteadily Maynard climbed to his feet. He headed for the nearest height. Before he reached it the second shattering roar came from the other side of the lagoon, and once again an ear-splitting explosion echoed from the vicinity of the rock. Maynard reached his vantage point and, through his binoculars, saw about a dozen men scurrying over the aft deck in and about the rear gun turret. A new and grimmer fury came against the camp director. He was determined that every man assisting on the destroyer must be arrested for malicious and dangerous trespass.

He did think vaguely that it was a sorry day indeed when inter-bureau squabbles could cause such open defiance of the armed forces, as if nothing more was involved than struggle for power. But that thought faded as swiftly as it came.

He waited for the third firing, then hurried down the hill to his camp. Swift commands to the men and officers sent eight of them to positions along the shore of the island, where they could watch boats trying to land. With the rest, Maynard headed towards the nearest navy boat. He had to take the long way around, by way of the point, and there must have been radio communication between the point and those on the ship, for a motor-boat was just appearing around the far end of the island when Maynard approached the now silent and deserted *Coulson*.

He hesitated. Should he give chase? A careful study of the rock proved it to be apparently unbroken. The failure cheered him, but also made him cautious. It wouldn't do for his superiors to discover that he had not taken the necessary precaution to prevent the destroyer being boarded.

He was still pondering the problem when Iilah started down the hill, straight towards the destroyer.

Iilah saw the first bright puff from the destroyer's guns. And then he had a moment during which he observed an object flash towards him. In the old, old times he had developed defences against hurtling objects. Quite automatically now, he tensed for the blow of this one. The object, instead of merely striking him with its hardness, exploded. The impact was stupendous. His protective crust cracked. The concussion blurred and distorted the flow from every electronic plate in his great mass.

Instantly, the automatic stabilizing 'tubes' sent out balancing impulses. The hot, internal, partly rigid, partly fluid matter that made up the greater portion of his body grew hotter, more fluidic. The weaknesses induced by that tremendous concussion accepted the natural union of a liquid, hardening quickly under enormous pressures. Sane again, Iilah considered what had happened. An attempt at communication?

The possibility excited him. Instead of closing the gap in his outer wall he hardened the matter immediately behind it, thus cutting off wasteful radiation. He waited. Again the hurtling object, and the enormously potent blow, as it struck him . . .

After a dozen blows, each with its resulting disaster to his protective shell, Iilah writhed with doubts. If these were messages he could not receive them, or understand. He began reluctantly to allow the chemical reactions that sealed the protective barrier. Faster than he could seal the holes, the hurtling objects breached his defences.

And still he did not think of what had happened as an attack. In all his previous existence he had never been attacked in such a fashion. Just what methods had been used against him Iilah could not remember. But certainly nothing so purely molecular.

The conviction that it was an attack came reluctantly, and he felt no anger. The reflex of defence in him was logical, not emotional. He studied the destroyer and it seemed to him that his purpose must be to drive it away. It would also be necessary to drive away every similar creature that tried to come near him. All the scurrying objects he had seen when he mounted the crest of the hill —all that must depart.

He started down the hill.

The creature floating above the plateau had ceased exuding flame. As Iilah eased himself near it, the only sign of life was a smaller object that darted alongside it.

There was a moment then when Iilah entered the water. That was a shock. He had almost forgotten that there was a level of this desolate mountain below which his life forces were affected.

He hesitated. Then, slowly, he slid further down into the depressing area, conscious that he had attained a level of strength that he could maintain against such a purely negative pressure.

The destroyer began to fire at him. The shells, delivered at point-blank range, poked deep holes into the ninety-foot cliff with which Iilah faced his enemy. As that wall of rock touched the destroyer, the firing stopped. (Maynard and his men, having defended the *Coulson* as long as possible, tumbled over the far side into their boat and raced away as fast as possible.)

Iilah shoved. The pain that he felt from those titanic blows was the pain that comes to all living creatures experiencing partial dissolution. Laboriously, his body repaired itself. And with anger and hatred and fear now, he shoved. In a few minutes he had tangled the curiously unwieldy structure in the rocks that rose up to form the edge of the plateau. Beyond was the sharp declining slope of the mountain.

An unexpected thing happened. Once among the rocks, the creature started to shudder and shake, as if caught by some inner destructive force. It fell over on its side and lay there like some wounded thing, quivering and breaking up.

It was an amazing spectacle. Iilah withdrew from the water, reclimbed the mountain, and plunged down into the sea on the other side, where a freighter was just getting under way. It swung around the promontory, and successfully floated through the channel and out, coasting along high above the bleak valley that fell away beyond the breakers. It moved along for several miles, then slowed and stopped.

Iilah would have liked to chase it further, but he was limited to ground movement. And so, the moment the freighter had stopped, he turned and headed towards the point, where the small objects were cluttered. He did not notice the men who plunged into the shallows near the shore and, from that comparative safety, watched the destruction of their equipment. Iilah left a wake of burning and crushed vehicles. The few drivers who tried to get their machines away became splotches of flesh and blood inside and on the metal of their machines.

There was a fantastic amount of stupidity and panic. Iilah moved at a speed of about eight miles an hour. Three hundred and seventeen men were caught in scores of individual traps and crushed by a monster that did not even know they existed. Each man must have felt himself personally pursued.

Afterwards, Iilah climbed to the nearest peak and studied the sky for further interlopers. Only the freighter remained, a shadowy threat some four miles away.

Darkness cloaked the island slowly. Maynard moved cautiously through the grass, flashing his flashlight directly in front of him on a sharp downward slant. Every little while he called out, 'Anybody around?' It had been like that for hours now. Through the fading day they had searched for survivors, each time loading them aboard their boat and ferrying them through the channel and out to where the freighter waited.

The orders had come through by radio. They had forty-eight hours to get clear of the island. After that the bomb run would be made by a drone plane.

Maynard pictured himself walking along on this monster-inhabited, night-enveloped island. And the shuddery thrill that came was almost pure unadulterated pleasure. He felt himself pale with a joyous terror. It was like the time his ship had been among those shelling a Jap-held beach. He had been gloomy until, suddenly, he had visualized himself out there on the beach at the receiving end of the shells. He began to torture himself with the possibility that, somehow, he might be left behind when the freighter finally withdrew.

A moan from the near darkness ended that thought. In the glow of the flashlight Maynard saw a vaguely familiar face. The man had been smashed by a falling tree. As executive officer Gerson came forward and administered morphine, Maynard bent closer to the injured man and peered at him anxiously.

It was one of the world-famous scientists on the island. Ever since the disaster the radio messages had been asking for him. There was not a scientific body on the globe that cared to commit itself to the navy bombing plan until he had given his opinion.

'Sir,' began Maynard, 'what do you think about——' He stopped. He settled mentally back on his heels.

Just for a moment he had forgotten that the naval authorities had already ordered the atomic bomb dropped, after being given governmental authority to do as they saw fit.

The scientist stirred. 'Maynard,' he croaked, 'there's something funny about that creature. Don't let them do any——' His eyes grew bright with pain. His voice trailed.

It was time to push questions. The great man would soon be deep in a doped sleep and he would be kept that way. In a moment it would be too late.

The moment passed.

Lieutenant Gerson climbed to his feet. 'There, that ought to do it, captain.' He turned to the seamen carrying the stretchers. 'Two of you take this man back to the boat. Careful. I've put him to sleep.'

Maynard followed the stretcher without a word. He had a sense of having been saved from the necessity of making a decision, rather than of having made one.

The night dragged on.

Morning dawned greyly. Shortly after the sun came up, a tropical shower stormed across the island and rushed off eastwards. The sky grew amazingly blue and the world of water all around seemed motionless, so calm did the sea become.

Out of the blue distance, casting a swiftly moving shadow on that still ocean, flew the drone plane. Long before it came in sight, Iilah sensed the load it carried. He quivered through his mass. Enormous electron tubes waxed and waned with expectancy and, for a brief while, he thought it was one of his own kind coming near.

As the plane drew closer he sent cautious thoughts towards it. Several planes, to which he had directed his thought waves, had twisted jerkily in mid-air and tumbled down out of control. But this one did not deviate from its course. When it was almost directly overhead a large object dropped from it, turned lazily over and over as it curved towards Iilah. It was set to explode about a hundred feet above the target.

The timing was perfect, the explosion titanic.

As soon as the blurring effects of so much new energy had passed, the now fully alive Iilah thought in a quiet, rather startled comprehension, 'Why, of course, that's what I was trying to remember. That's what I was supposed to do.'

He was puzzled that he could have forgotten. He had been sent during the course of an interstellar war—which apparently was still going on. He had been dropped on the planet under enormous difficulties and had been instantly snuffed out by enemy frustrators. Now he was ready to do his job.

He took test sightings on the sun and on the planets that were within reach of his radar signals. Then he set in motion an orderly process that would dissolve all the shields inside his own body. He gathered his pressure forces for the final thrust that would bring the vital elements hard together at exactly the calculated moment.

The explosion that knocked a planet out of its orbit was recorded on every seismograph on the globe. It would be some time, however, before astronomers would discover that earth was falling into the sun. And no man would live to see Sol flare into Nova brightness, and burn up the Solar System before gradually sinking back into a dim G state.

Even if Iilah had known that it was not the same war that had raged ten thousand million centuries before, he would have had no choice but to do as he did.

Robot atom bombs do not make up their own minds.

THE SEA RAIDERS

H. G. WELLS

I

UNTIL THE extraordinary affair at Sidmouth, the peculiar species *Haploteuthis ferox* was known to science only generically, on the strength of a half-digested tentacle obtained near the Azores, and a decaying body pecked by birds and nibbled by fish, found early in 1896 by Mr. Jennings, near Land's End.

In no department of zoological science, indeed, are we quite so much in the dark as with regard to the deep-sea cephalopods. A mere accident, for instance, it was that led to the Prince of Monaco's discovery of nearly a dozen new forms in the summer of 1895, a discovery in which the before-mentioned tentacle was included. It chanced that a cachalot was killed off Terceira by some sperm whalers, and in its last struggles charged almost to the Prince's yacht, missed it, rolled under, and died within twenty yards of his rudder. And in its agony it threw up a number of large objects, which the Prince, dimly perceiving they were strange and important, was, by a happy expedient, able to secure before they sank. He set his screws in motion, and kept them circling in the vortices thus created until a boat could be lowered. And these specimens were whole cephalopods and fragments of cephalopods, some of gigantic proportions, and almost all of them unknown to science!

It would seem, indeed, that these large and agile creatures, living in the middle depths of the sea, must, to a large extent, for ever remain unknown to us, since under water they are too nimble for nets, and it is only by such rare, unlooked-for accidents that specimens can be obtained. In the case of *Haploteuthis ferox*, for instance, we are still altogether ignorant of its habitat, as ignorant as we are of the breeding-ground of the herring or the sea-ways of the salmon. And zoologists are altogether at a loss to account for its sudden appearance on our coast. Possibly it was the stress of a hunger migration that drove it hither out of the deep. But it will be, perhaps, better to avoid necessarily inconclusive discussion, and to proceed at once with our narrative.

The first human being to set eyes upon a living *Haploteuthis*—the first human being to survive, that is, for there can be little doubt now that the wave of bathing fatalities and boating accidents that travelled along the coast of Cornwall and Devon in early May was due to this cause—was a retired tea-dealer of the name of Fison, who was stopping at a Sidmouth boarding-house. It was in the afternoon, and he was walking along the cliff path between Sidmouth and Ladram Bay. The cliffs in this direction are very high, but down the red face of them in one place a kind of ladder staircase has been made. He was near this when his attention was attracted by what at first he thought to be a cluster of birds struggling over a fragment of food that caught the sunlight, and glistened pinkish-white. The tide was right out, and this object was not only far below him, but remote across a broad waste of rock reef covered with dark seaweed and interspersed with silvery shining tidal pools. And he was, moreover, dazzled by the brightness of the further water.

In a minute, regarding this again, he perceived that his judgment was in fault, for over this struggle circled a number of birds, jackdaws and gulls, for the most part, the latter gleaming blindingly when the sunlight smote their

L

wings, and they seemed minute in comparison with it. And his curiosity was, perhaps, aroused all the more strongly because of his first insufficient explanations.

As he had nothing better to do than amuse himself, he decided to make this object, whatever it was, the goal of his afternoon walk, instead of Ladram Bay, conceiving it might perhaps be a great fish of some sort, stranded by some chance, and flapping about in its distress. And so he hurried down the long steep ladder, stopping at intervals of thirty feet or so to take breath and scan the mysterious movement.

At the foot of the cliff he was, of course, nearer his object than he had been; but, on the other hand, it now came up against the incandescent sky, beneath the sun, so as to seem dark and indistinct. Whatever was pinkish of it was now hidden by a skerry of weedy boulders. But he perceived that it was made up of seven rounded bodies, distinct or connected, and that the birds kept up a constant croaking and screaming, but seemed afraid to approach it too closely.

Mr. Fison, torn by curiosity, began picking his way across the wave-worn rocks and finding the wet sea-weed that covered them thickly rendered them extremely slippery, he stopped, removed his shoes and socks, and coiled his trousers above his knees. His object was, of course, merely to avoid stumbling into the rocky pools about him, and perhaps he was rather glad, as all men are, of an excuse to resume, even for a moment, the sensations of his boyhood. At any rate, it is to this, no doubt, that he owes his life.

He approached his mark with all the assurance which the absolute security of this country against all forms of animal life gives its inhabitants. The round bodies moved to and fro, but it was only when he surmounted the skerry of boulders I have mentioned that he realized the horrible nature of the discovery. It came upon him with some suddenness.

The rounded bodies fell apart as he came in to sight over the ridge, and displayed the pinkish object to be the partially devoured body of a human being, but whether of a man or woman he was unable to say. And the rounded bodies were new and ghastly-looking creatures, in shape somewhat resembling an octopus, and with huge and very long and flexible tentacles, coiled copiously on the ground. The skin had a glistening texture, unpleasant to see, like shiny leather. The downward bend of the tentacle-surrounded mouth, the curious excrescence at the bend, the tentacles, and the large intelligent eyes, gave the creatures a grotesque suggestion of a face. They were the size of a fair-sized swine about the body, and the tentacles seemed to him to be many feet in length. There were, he thinks, seven or eight at least of the creatures. Twenty yards beyond them, amid the surf of the now returning tide, two others were emerging from the sea.

Their bodies lay flatly on the rocks, and their eyes regarded him with evil interest; but it does not appear that Mr. Fison was afraid, or that he realized that he was in any danger. Possibly his confidence is to be ascribed to the limpness of their attitudes. But he was horrified, of course, and intensely excited and indignant, at such revolting creatures preying upon human flesh. He thought they had chanced upon a drowned body. He shouted to them, with the idea of driving them off, and finding they did not budge, cast about him, picked up a big rounded lump of rock, and flung it at one.

And then, slowly uncoiling their tentacles, they all began moving towards him—creeping at first deliberately, and making a soft purring sound to each other.

In a moment Mr. Fison realized that he was in danger. He shouted again, threw both his boots, and started off, with a leap, forthwith. Twenty yards off he stopped and faced about, judging them slow, and behold! the tentacles of their leader were already pouring over the rocky ridge on which he had just been standing!

At that he shouted again, but this time not threatening, but a cry of dismay, and began jumping, striding, slipping, wading across the uneven expanse between him and the beach. The tall red cliffs seemed suddenly at a vast distance, and he saw, as though they were creatures in another world, two minute workmen engaged in the repair of the ladder-way, and little suspecting the race for life that was beginning below them. At one time he could hear the creatures splashing in the pools not a dozen feet behind him, and once he slipped and almost fell.

They chased him to the very foot of the cliffs, and desisted only when he had been joined by the workmen at the foot of the ladder-way up the cliff. All three of the men pelted them with stones for a time, and then hurried to the cliff top and along the path towards Sidmouth, to secure assistance and a boat, and to rescue the desecrated body from the clutches of these abominable creatures.

II

AND, as if he had not already been in sufficient peril that day, Mr. Fison went with the boat to point out the exact spot of his adventure.

As the tide was down, it required a considerable detour to reach the spot, and when at last they came off the ladder-way, the mangled body had disappeared. The water was now running in, submerging first one slab of slimy rock and then another, and the four men in the boat—the workmen, that is, the boatman, and Mr. Fison—now turned their attention from the bearings off shore to the water beneath the keel.

At first they could see little below them, save a dark jungle of laminaria, with an occasional darting fish. Their minds were set on adventure, and they expressed their disappointment freely. But presently they saw one of the monsters swimming through the water seaward, with a curious rolling motion that suggested to Mr. Fison the spinning roll of a captive balloon. Almost immediately after, the waving streamers of laminaria were extraordinarily perturbed, parted for a moment, and three of these beasts became darkly visible, struggling for what was probably some fragment of the drowned man. In a moment the copious olive-green ribbons had poured again over this writhing group.

At that all four men, greatly excited, began beating the water with oars and shouting, and immediately they saw a tumultuous movement among the weeds. They desisted to see more clearly, and as soon as the water was smooth, they saw, as it seemed to them, the whole sea bottom among the weeds set with eyes.

'Ugly swine!' cried one of the men. 'Why, there's dozens!'

And forthwith the things began to rise through the water about them. Mr. Fison has since described to the writer this startling eruption out of the waving laminaria meadows. To him it seemed to occupy a considerable time, but it is probable that really it was an affair of a few seconds only. For a time nothing but eyes, and then he speaks of tentacles streaming out and parting the weed fronds this way and that. Then these things, growing larger, until at last the bottom was hidden by their intercoiling forms, and the tips of tentacles rose darkly here and there into the air above the swell of the waters.

One came up boldly to the side of the boat, and clinging to this with three of its sucker-set tentacles, threw four others over the gunwhale, as if with an intention either of oversetting the boat or of clambering into it. Mr. Fison at once caught up the boat-hook, and, jabbing furiously at the soft tentacles, forced it to desist. He was struck in the back and almost pitched overboard by the boatman, who was using his oar to resist a similar attack on the other side of the boat. But the tentacles on either side at once relaxed their hold at this, slid out of sight, and splashed into the water.

'We'd better get out of this,' said Mr. Fison, who was trembling violently. He went to the tiller, while the boat-man and one of the workmen seated themselves and began rowing. The other workman stood up in the fore part of the boat, with the boat-hook, ready to strike any more tentacles that might appear. Nothing else seems to have been said. Mr. Fison had expressed the common feeling be-yond amendment. In a hushed, scared mood, with faces white and drawn, they set about escaping from the posi-tion into which they had so recklessly blundered.

But the oars had scarcely dropped into the water before dark, tapering, serpentine ropes had bound them, and were about the rudder; and creeping up the sides of the boat with a looping motion came the suckers again. The men gripped their oars and pulled, but it was like trying to move a boat in a floating raft of weeds. 'Help here!' cried the boatman, and Mr. Fison and the second workman rushed to help lug at the oar.

Then the man with the boat-hook—his name was Ewan, or Ewen—sprang up with a curse and began striking down-ward over the side, as far as he could reach, at the bank of tentacles that now clustered along the boat's bottom. And, at the same time, the two rowers stood up to get a better purchase for the recovery of their oars. The boat-man handed his to Mr. Fison, who lugged desperately, and, meanwhile, the boatman opened a big clasp-knife, and lean-ing over the side of the boat, began hacking at the spiring arms upon the oar shaft.

Mr. Fison, staggering with the quivering rocking of the boat, his teeth set, his breath coming short, and the veins starting on his hands as he pulled at his oar, suddenly cast his eyes seaward. And there, not fifty yards off, across the long rollers of the incoming tide, was a large boat stand-ing in towards them, with three women and a little child in it. A boatman was rowing, and a little man with a pink-ribboned straw hat and whites stood in the stern hailing them. For a moment, of course, Mr. Fison thought of help, and then he thought of the child. He abandoned his oar forthwith, threw up his arms in a frantic gesture, and screamed to the party in the boat to keep away 'for God's sake!'

It says much for the modesty and courage of Mr. Fison that he does not seem to be aware that there was any quality of heroism in his action at this juncture. The oar he had abandoned was at once drawn under, and presently reappeared floating about twenty yards away.

At the same moment Mr. Fison felt the boat under him lurch violently, and a hoarse scream, a prolonged cry of terror from Hill, the boatman, caused him to forget the party of excursionists altogether. He turned, and saw Hill crouching by the forward row-lock, his face convulsed with terror, and his right arm over the side and drawn tightly down. He gave now a succession of short, sharp cries, 'Oh! oh! oh!—oh!' Mr. Fison believes that he must have been hacking at the tentacles below the water-line, and have been grasped by them, but, of course, it is quite impossible to say now certainly what had happened. The boat was heeling over, so that the gunwhale was within ten inches of the water, and both Ewan and the other labourer were striking down into the water, with oar and boat-hook, on either side of Hill's arm. Mr. Fison instinctively placed himself to counterpoise them.

Then Hill, who was a burly, powerful man, made a strenuous effort, and rose almost to a standing position. He lifted his arm, indeed, clean out of the water. Hanging to it was a complicated tangle of brown ropes, and the eyes of one of the brutes that had hold of him, glaring straight and resolute, showed momentarily above the surface. The boat heeled more and more, and the green-brown water came pouring in a cascade over the side. Then Hill slipped and fell with his ribs across the side, and his arm and the mass of tentacles about it splashed back into the water.

He rolled over; his boot kicked Mr. Fison's knee as that gentleman rushed forward to seize him, and in another moment fresh tentacles had whipped about his waist and neck, and after a brief, convulsive struggle, in which the boat was nearly capsized, Hill was lugged overboard. The boat righted with a violent jerk that all but sent Mr. Fison over the other side, and hid the struggle in the water from his eyes.

He stood staggering to recover his balance for a moment, and as he did so he became aware that the struggle and the inflowing tide had carried them close upon the weedy rocks again. Not four yards off a table of rock still rose in rhythmic movements above the inwash of the tide. In a moment Mr. Fison seized the oar from Ewan, gave one vigorous stroke, then dropping it, ran to the bows and leapt. He felt his feet slide over the rock, and, by a frantic effort, leapt again towards a further mass. He stumbled over this, came to his knees, and rose again.

'Look out!' cried some one, and a large drab body struck him. He was knocked flat into a tidal pool by one of the workmen, and as he went down he heard smothered, chok-ing cries, that he believed at the time came from Hill. Then he found himself marvelling at the shrillness and variety of Hill's voice. Some one jumped over him, and a curving rush of foamy water poured over him, and passed. He scrambled to his feet, dripping, and, without looking seaward, ran as fast as his terror would let him, shoreward. Before him, over the flat space of scattered rocks, stumbled the two workmen—one a dozen yards in front of the other.

He looked over his shoulder at last, and seeing that he was not pursued, faced about. He was astonished. From the moment of the rising of the cephalopods out of the water he had been acting too swiftly to fully comprehend his actions. Now it seemed to him as if he had suddenly jumped out of an evil dream.

For there were the sky, cloudless and blazing with the afternoon sun, the sea weltering under its pitiless brightness, the soft creamy foam of the breaking water, and the low, long, dark ridges of rock. The righted boat floated, rising and falling gently on the swell about a dozen yards from shore. Hill and the monsters, all the stress and tumult of that fierce fight for life, had vanished as though they had never been.

Mr. Fison's heart was beating violently; he was throbbing to the finger-tips, and his breath came deep.

There was something missing. For some seconds he could not think clearly enough what this might be. Sun, sky, sea, rocks—what was it? Then he remembered the boat-load of excursionists. It had vanished. He wondered whether he had imagined it. He turned, and saw the two workmen standing side by side under the projecting masses of the tall pink cliffs. He hesitated whether he should make one last attempt to save the man Hill. His physical excitement seemed to desert him suddenly, and leave him aimless and helpless. He turned shoreward, stumbling and wading towards his two companions.

He looked back again, and there were now two boats floating, and the one farthest out at sea pitched clumsily, bottom upward.

III

So it was *Haploteuthis ferox* made its appearance upon the Devonshire coast. So far, this has been its most serious aggression. Mr. Fison's account, taken together with the wave of boating and bathing casualties to which I have already alluded, and the absence of fish from the Cornish coasts that year, points clearly to a shoal of these voracious deep-sea monsters prowling slowly along the sub-tidal coast-line. Hunger migration has, I know, been suggested as the force that drove them hither; but, for my own part, I prefer to believe the alternative theory of Hemsley. Hemsley holds that a pack or shoal of these creatures may have become enamoured of human flesh by the accident of a foundered ship sinking among them, and have wandered in search of it out of their accustomed zone; first waylaying and following ships, and so coming to our shores in the wake of the Atlantic traffic. But to discuss Hemsley's cogent and admirably-stated arguments would be out of place here.

It would seem that the appetites of the shoal were satisfied by the catch of eleven people—for, so far as can be ascertained, there were ten people in the second boat, and certainly these creatures gave no further signs of their presence off Sidmouth that day. The coast between Seaton and Budleigh Salterton was patrolled all that evening and night by four Preventive Service boats, the men in which were armed with harpoons and cutlasses, and as the evening advanced, a number of more or less similarly equipped expeditions, organized by private individuals, joined them. Mr. Fison took no part in any of these expeditions.

About midnight excited hails were heard from a boat about a couple of miles out at sea to the south-east of Sidmouth, and a lantern was seen waving in a strange manner to and fro and up and down. The nearer boats at once hurried towards the alarm. The venturesome occupants of the boat—a seaman, a curate, and two schoolboys—had actually seen the monsters passing under their boat. The creatures, it seems, like most deep-sea organisms, were phosphorescent, and they had been floating, five fathoms deep or so, like creatures of moonshine through the blackness of the water, their tentacles retracted and as if asleep, rolling over and over, and moving slowly in a wedge-like formation towards the south-east.

These people told their story in gesticulated fragments, as first one boat drew alongside and then another. At last there was a little fleet of eight or nine boats collected together, and from them a tumult, like the chatter of a market-place, rose into the stillness of the night. There was little or no disposition to pursue the shoal, the people had neither weapons nor experience for such a dubious chase, and presently—even with a certain relief, it may be—the boats turned shoreward.

And now to tell what is perhaps the most astonishing fact in this whole astonishing raid. We have not the slightest knowledge of the subsequent movements of the shoal, although the whole south-west coast was now alert for it. But it may, perhaps, be significant that a cachalot was stranded off Sark on June 3. Two weeks and three days after this Sidmouth affair, a living *Haploteuthis* came ashore on Calais sands. It was alive, because several witnesses saw its tentacles moving in a convulsive way. But it is probable that it was dying. A gentleman named Pouchet obtained a rifle and shot it.

That was the last appearance of a living *Haploteuthis*. No others were seen on the French coast. On the 15th of June a dead carcass, almost complete, was washed ashore near Torquay, and a few days later a boat from the Marine Biological station, engaged in dredging off Plymouth, picked up a rotting specimen, slashed deeply with a cutlass wound. How the former had come by its death it is impossible to say. And on the last day of June, Mr. Egbert Caine, an artist, bathing near Newlyn, threw up his arms, shrieked, and was drawn under. A friend bathing with him made no attempt to save him, but swam at once for the shore. This is the last fact to tell of this extraordinary raid from the deeper sea. Whether it is really the last of these horrible creatures, it is, as yet, premature to say. But it is believed, and certainly it is to be hoped, that they have returned now, and returned for good, to the sunless depths of the middle seas, out of which they have so strangely and so mysteriously arisen.

DUMB SHOW

BRIAN W. ALDISS

MRS. SNOWDEN was slowly being worn down. She had reached the stage now where she carried about with her a square of card on which the word DON'T was written in large letters. It was kept tucked inside her cardigan, ready to be produced at a moment's notice and flashed before Pauline's eyes.

The ill-matched pair, the grubby girl of three and the shabby-elegant lady of fifty-eight, came up to the side door of their house, Pauline capering over the flagstones, Mrs. Snowden walking slowly with her eyes on the bare border. Spring was reluctantly here, but the tepid earth hardly acknowledged it; even the daffodils had failed to put in an appearance this year.

'Can't understand it at all,' Mrs. Snowden told herself. 'Nothing ever happens to daffodils.' And then she went on to compile a list of things that nevertheless might have happened : frost—it had been a hard winter; soil-starvation —no manure since the outbreak of hostilities, seven years ago; ants; mice; cats; the sounds—that seemed most likely. Sound did anything, these days.

Pauline rapped primly on the little brass knocker and vanished into the hall. Mrs. Snowden paused in the porch, stopping to look back at the houses on the other side of her high brick wall. When this house had been built, it had stood in open fields; now drab little semi-detacheds surrounded it on three sides. She paused and hated them. Catching herself at it, she tried instead to admire the late afternoon light falling on the huddled roofs; the sunshine fell in languid, horizontal strokes—but it had no meaning for her, except as a sign that it was nearly time to blackout again.

She went heavily into the house, closing the door. Inside, night had already commenced.

Her granddaughter marched round the drawing-room, banging a tin lid against her head. That way, she could hear the noise it made. Mrs. Snowden reached for the DON'T card, then let her hand drop; the action was becoming automatic, and she must guard against it. She went to the gram-wire-tv cabinet, of which only the last compartment was now of use, and switched on. Conditions at home were a little better since the recapture of Iceland, and there were now broadcasts for an hour and a half every evening.

Circuits warmed, a picture burned in the half-globe. A man and woman danced solemnly, without music. To Mrs. Snowden it looked as meaningless as turning a book of blank pages, but Pauline stopped her march and came to stare. She smiled at the dancing couple; her lips moved; she was talking to them.

DON'T, screamed Mrs. Snowden's sudden, dumb card.

Pauline made a face and answered back. She jumped away as her grandmother reached forward, leaping, prancing over the chairs, shouting defiance.

In fury, Mrs. Snowden skimmed the card across the room, crying angrily, hating to be reminded of her infirmity, waving her narrow hands. She collapsed on to a music stool—music, that dear, extinct thing!—and wept. Her own anger in her own head had sounded a million cotton-wool miles away, emphasizing the isolation. At this point she always crumpled.

The little girl came to her delicately, treading and staring with impertinence, knowing she had the victory. She pulled a sweet face and twizzled on her heel. Lack of hearing did not worry her; the silence she had known in the womb had never left her. Her indifference seemed a mockery.

'You little beast!' Mrs. Snowden said. 'You cruel, ignorant, little beast!'

Pauline replied, the little babblings which would never turn into words, the little noises no human ear could hear. Then she walked quietly over to the windows, pointed out at the sickening day, and began to draw the curtains. Controlling herself with an effort, Mrs. Snowden stood up. Thank goodness the child had some sense; they must blackout. First she retrieved her DON'T card from behind the ancient twentieth-century settee, and then they went together through the house, tugging the folds of black velvet across the glass.

Now Pauline was skipping again. How she did it on the low calories was a matter for wonder. Perhaps, thought Mrs. Snowden, it was a blessing to be responsible for the child; so, she kept contact with life. She even caught an echo of gaiety herself, so that they hurried from room to room like bearers of good news, pulling blackness over them, then sweeping on the sonic lights. Up the stairs, pausing at the landing window, racing into the bedrooms, till new citadels were created from all the shabby darknesses. Pauline collapsed laughing on her bed. Seizing her, tickling now and again, Mrs. Snowden undressed her and tucked her between the fraying sheets.

She kissed the girl good night, put out the light, closed the door, and then went slowly round, putting out all the other lights, downstairs, putting all the lights out there.

Directly she had gone, Pauline climbed out of bed, stamped into the bathroom, opened the little medicine cupboard, took out the bottle with the label 'Sleeping Pills'. Unscrewing the top, she swallowed a pill, pulling a pig's eyes face at herself in the looking-glass as she did so. Then she put the bottle back on its shelf and slammed the little door, hugging to herself this noisy secret.

None of these things had names for her. Having no
names, they had only misty meanings. The very edges of
them were blurred, for all objects were grouped together in
only two vast categories: those-that-concerned-her and
those-that-did-not-concern-her.

She trailed loudly back to her bed in the silence there
was no breaking, making pig's eyes all the way to ward off
the darkness. Once in bed, she began to think; it was because of these pictures she stole her grandmother's pills:
they fought the pictures and turned them eventually into
an all-night nothing.

Predominant was the aching picture. A warmth. a face.
a comforting—it was at once the vaguest yet most vivid
picture; someone soft who carried and cared for her; someone who now never came; someone who now provoked
only the water scalding from her eyes.

Elbowing that picture away came the boring picture.
This tall, old-smelling person who had suddenly become
everything after the other had gone; her stiff fingers, bad
over buttons; her slowness about the stove; her meaningless
marks on cards; all the dull mystery of who she was and
what she did.

The new picture. The room down the road where Pauline
was taken every morning. It was full of small people, some
like her, in frocks, some with short hair and fierce movements. And big people, walking between their seats,
again with marks on cards, trying with despairing faces
to make them comprehend incomprehensible things by
gestures of the hand and fingers.

The push picture. Something needed, strange as sunlight,
something lost, lost as laughter. . . .

The pill worked like a time-bomb and Pauline was asleep
where only the neurosis of puzzlement could insidiously
follow.

Mrs. Snowden switched the globe off and sank into a
chair. They had been showing a silent film: the latest

scientific advances had thrown entertainment back to where it had been in her grandfather's young days. For a moment she had watched the silent gestures, followed by a wall of dialogue:

'Jean: Then—you knew he was not my father, Denis?

'Denis: From the first moment we met in Madrid.

'Jean: And I swore none should ever know.'

Sighing, Mrs. Snowden switched the poor stuff off, and sank down with a hand over her forehead. TV merely accentuated her isolation, everyone's isolation. She thought mockingly of the newspaper phrase describing this conflict, The Civilized War, and wished momentarily for one of the old, rough kind with doodlebugs and H-bombs; then you could achieve a sort of Henry Moore-ish anonymity, crouching with massed others underground. Now, your individuality was forced on to you, till self-consciousness became a burden that sunk you in an ocean of loneliness.

Right at the beginning of this war, Mrs. Snowden's husband had left for the duration. He was on secret work—where, she had no idea. Up till two years ago, she received a card from him each Christmas; then he had missed a year; then, in the paper shortage, the sending of cards had been forbidden. So whether he lived or not she did not know; the question now raised curiously little excitement in her. Heart-sickness had ceased to be relevant.

Mrs. Snowden had come to live here in her old home with her parents after she had been declared redundant at the university, when all but the practical Chairs closed down. In the lean winters, first her mother then her father died. Then her married daughter was killed in a sound raid; Pauline, a tiny babe, had come to live with her.

It was all impersonal, dry facts, she thought. You stated the facts to explain how the situation arose; but to explain the *situation*. . . .

Nobody in the world could hear a sound. *That* was the only important fact.

She jumped up and flicked aside an edge of curtain. A rag of dirty daylight was still propped over the serried chimney-tops. The more those houses crowded, the more they isolated her. This should be a time for madness, she said aloud, misting the pane : something grand and horrid to break the chain of days. And her eyes swept the treble row of old textbooks over her bureau : Jackson's *Eighteen Nineties*, Montgomery's *Early Twentieth Century Science Fiction*, Slade's *Novelists of the Psychological Era*, Wilson's *Zola*, Nolleybend's *Wilson* . . . a row of dodos, as defunct as the courses of Eng. Lit. they had once nourished.

'Dead!' she exclaimed. 'A culture in Coventry!' she whispered, and went to get something to eat.

'Tough old hag,' she told herself. 'You'll survive.'

The food was the usual vibro-culture, tasteless, filling, insubstantial. The hospitals of England held as many beri-beri cases as wounded. Sound ruled the whole deaf world. It wrecked the buildings, killed the soldiers, shattered the tympanums and ballooned synthesized proteins from mixtures of animo acids.

The Sound Revolution had come at the dawn of this new century, following thirty years of peace. Progress had taken a new direction. It had all been simple and complete; you just flushed the right electrostatic stress through the right quartz plates and—bingo! You could do anything! The most spectacular result was a global conflict.

The Powers warred under certain humane agreements : gas, fission and fusion weapons were forbidden. It was to be, indeed, a Civilized War. VM (vibratory motion) had the field to itself. It learnt to expand living vegetable cells a thousand-fold, so that a potato would last for two years' dinners; it learnt to pulverize brick and metal, so that cities could comfortably be turned to a thin dust; it learnt to twist the human ear into an echoing, useless coil of gristle. There seemed no limit to its adaptability.

Mrs. Snowden ate her blown-up yeast with dignity, and thought of other things. She thought—for lately she had

M

been straining after wider horizons—of the course of human history, its paradoxical sameness and variety, and then something made her look up to the tube over the mantelpiece.

The tube was a piece of standard equipment in every home. It was a crude ear, designed to announce when the local siren was giving a sound raid alarm.

She glanced indifferently at it. The lycopodium seed was stirring sluggishly in its tube; damp must be getting in, it was not patterning properly. She went on eating, gloomily wondering about the future generations: how much of the vital essence of tradition would be lost through this blanket of deafness?

Correct procedure would have been for her, at the stirring of the seed, to collect Pauline and stand out in the open. When the siren went, everyone else left their homes and stood patiently under the bare sky; then, if the sounds swept their buildings, they would be temporarily smothered by dust as the building vanished, but suffer no other harm. Mrs. Snowden could no longer be bothered with this nonsense.

To her mind, it was undignified to stand in the chill air, meekly waiting. If enemy planes circled overhead, she would have had defiance to spur her out; but nowadays there was only the quiet sky, the eternal silence and the abrupt pulverization—or the anti-climax, when everyone filed sheepishly back to bed.

She took her plate into the kitchen. As she came back into the living-room, a reproduction of Mellor's 'Egyptian Girl' fell silently on to the floor, shattering frame and glass.

Mrs. Snowden went and stared at it. Then, on impulse, she hurried over to the window and peered out. The encircling houses had gone.

Letting the curtain fall back into place, she rushed from the room and up the stairs. She was shaking Pauline before she regained control of herself, and then could not tell whether panic or exultation had sent her scurrying.

'The houses have gone! The houses have gone!'

Silence, in which the little girl woke sluggishly.

Mrs. Snowden hustled her downstairs and out on to the front lawn, letting a bright swathe of light cut across the empty flower-beds. Somewhere, high and silent overhead, a monitor might be hovering, but she was too excited to care.

By a freak of chance, their house stood alone. Around them for miles stretched a new desert, undulant, still settling. The novelty, the *difference*, of it was something wonderful: not a catastrophe, a liberation.

Then they saw the giants.

Vague in the distance, they were nevertheless real enough, although incredible. They were tall—how tall? —ten, fifteen feet? More? With horror Mrs. Snowden thought they were enemy troops. This was the latest application of the sound: it enlarged the human cell now, as easily as it enlarged vegetable cells. She had the brief idea she had read that human giants could not survive, or were impossible or something, and then the thought was gone, swept away in fear.

The giants were still growing. They were taller than a house now, thirty feet or more high. They began to mop and mow, like drunken dancers.

Unreality touched her. Pauline was crying.

A coolness swept her limbs. She trembled involuntarily. A personal alarm now, terror because something unknown was at her blood. She raised a hand to her eyes. It loomed away from her. Her arm extended. She was *growing*.

She knew then that the giants were no enemy troops; they were victims. You get everyone out of their houses. One type of VM levels the houses. Another inflates the people, blowing them up like grotesque rubber dummies. Simple. Scientific. Civilized.

Mrs. Snowden swayed like a pole. She took a clumsy step to keep her balance. Dizzily, she peered at her blank bedroom window, staggering away to avoid falling into the house. No pain. The circuits were disrupted. Only numbness: numbness and maniac growth.

She could still crazily see the dancing giants. Now she understood why they danced. They were trying to adapt. Before they could do so, their metabolism burnt out. They sprawled into the desert, giant dusty corpses, full of sound and silence.

She thought: It's the first excitement for years, amusedly, before her heart failed under its giant load.

She toppled; the DON'T card fluttered gaily from her bosom, spinning and filtering to the ground.

Pauline had already overtopped her grandmother. The young system was greedy for growth. She uttered a cry of wonder as her head rocked up to the dark sky. She saw her grandmother fall. She saw the tiny fan of sonic light from their tiny front door. She trod into the desert to keep her balance. She started to run. She saw the ground dwindle. She felt the warmth of the stars, the curvature of the earth.

In her brain, the delighted thoughts were wasps in a honey pot, bees in a hive, flies in a chapel, gnats in a factory, midges in a Sahara, sparks up an everlasting flue, a comet falling for ever in a noiseless void, a voice singing in a new universe.

THE NINE BILLION NAMES ·OF GOD

ARTHUR C. CLARKE

'THIS IS a slightly unusual request,' said Dr. Wagner, with what he hoped was commendable restraint. 'As far as I know, it's the first time anyone's been asked to supply a Tibetan monastery with an Automatic Sequence Computer. I don't wish to be inquisitive, but I should hardly have thought that your—ah—establishment had much use for such a machine. Could you explain just what you intend to do with it?'

'Gladly,' replied the Lama, readjusting his silk robe and carefully putting away the slide rule he had been using for currency conversions. 'Your Mark V Computer can carry out any routine mathematical operation involving up to ten digits. However, for our work we are interested in *letters*, not numbers. As we wish you to modify the output circuits, the machine will be printing words, not columns of figures.'

'I don't quite understand . . .'

'This is a project on which we have been working for the last three centuries—since the lamasery was founded, in fact. It is somewhat alien to your way of thought, so I hope you will listen with an open mind while I explain it.'

'Naturally.'

'It is really quite simple. We have been compiling a list which shall contain all the possible names of God.'

'I beg your pardon?'

'We have reason to believe,' continued the Lama imperturbably, 'that all such names can be written with not more than nine letters in an alphabet we have devised.'

'And you have been doing this for three centuries?'

'Yes: we expected it would take us about fifteen thousand years to complete the task.'

'Oh.' Dr. Wagner looked a little dazed. 'Now I see why you wanted to hire one of our machines. But exactly what is the *purpose* of this project?'

The Lama hesitated for a fraction of a second and Wagner wondered if he had offended him. If so, there was no trace of annoyance in the reply.

'Call it ritual, if you like, but it's a fundamental part of our belief. All the many names of the Supreme Being— God, Jehovah, Allah, and so on—they are only man-made labels. There is a philosophical problem of some difficulty here, which I do not propose to discuss, but somewhere among all the possible combinations of letters which can occur are what one may call the *real* names of God. By systematic permutation of letters, we have been trying to list them all.'

'I see. You've been starting at AAAAAAAAA . . . and working up to ZZZZZZZZZ . . .'

'Exactly—though we use a special alphabet of our own. Modifying the electromatic typewriters to deal with this is, of course, trivial. A rather more interesting problem is that of devising suitable circuits to eliminate ridiculous combinations. For example, no letter must occur more than three times in succession.'

'Three? Surely you mean two.'

'Three is correct: I am afraid it would take too long to explain why, even if you understood our language.'

'I'm sure it would,' said Wagner hastily. 'Go on.'

'Luckily, it will be a simple matter to adapt your Automatic Sequence Computer for this work, since once it has been programmed properly it will permute each letter in turn and print the result. What would have taken us fifteen thousand years it will be able to do in a hundred days.'

Dr. Wagner was scarcely conscious of the faint sounds from the Manhattan streets far below. He was in a different world, a world of natural, not man-made mountains. High up in their remote aeries these monks had been patiently at work, generation after generation, compiling their lists of meaningless words. Was there any limit to the follies of mankind? Still, he must give no hint of his inner thoughts. The customer was always right . . .

'There's no doubt,' replied the doctor, 'that we can modify the Mark V to print lists of this nature. I'm much more worried about the problem of installation and maintenance. Getting out to Tibet, in these days, is not going to be easy.'

'We can arrange that. The components are small enough to travel by air—that is one reason why we chose your machine. If you can get them to India, we will provide transport from there.'

'And you want to hire two of our engineers?'

'Yes, for the three months which the project should occupy.'

'I've no doubt that Personnel can manage that.' Dr. Wagner scribbled a note on his desk pad. 'There are just two other points——'

Before he could finish the sentence the Lama had produced a small slip of paper.

'This is my certified credit balance at the Asiatic Bank.'

'Thank you. It appears to be—ah—adequate. The second matter is so trivial that I hesitate to mention it—but it's surprising how often the obvious gets overlooked. What source of electrical energy have you?'

'A diesel generator providing 50 kilowatts at 110 volts. It was installed about five years ago and is quite reliable. It's made life at the lamasery much more comfortable, but of course it was really installed to provide power for the motors driving the prayer wheels.'

'Of course,' echoed Dr. Wagner. 'I should have thought of that.'

The view from the parapet was vertiginous, but in time one gets used to anything. After three months, George Hanley was not impressed by the two-thousand-foot swoop into the abyss or the remote checkerboard of fields in the valley below. He was leaning against the wind-smoothed stones and staring morosely at the distant mountains whose names he had never bothered to discover.

This, thought George, was the craziest thing that had ever happened to him. 'Project Shangri-La,' some wit at the labs had christened it. For weeks now the Mark V had been churning out acres of sheets covered with gibberish. Patiently, inexorably, the computer had been rearranging letters in all their possible combinations, exhausting each class before going on to the next. As the sheets had emerged from the electromatic typewriters, the monks had carefully cut them up and pasted them into enormous books. In another week, heaven be praised, they would have finished. Just what obscure calculations had convinced the monks that they needn't bother to go on to words of ten, twenty or a hundred letters, George didn't know. One of his recurring nightmares was that there would be some change of plan, and that the High Lama (whom they'd naturally called Sam Jaffe, though he didn't look a bit like him) would suddenly announce that the project would be extended to approximately A.D. 2060. They were quite capable of it.

George heard the heavy wooden door slam in the wind as Chuck came out on to the parapet beside him. As usual, Chuck was smoking one of the cigars that made him so popular with the monks—who, it seemed, were quite willing to embrace all the minor and most of the major pleasures of life. That was one thing in their favour: they might be crazy, but they weren't bluenoses. Those frequent trips they took down to the village, for instance . . .

'Listen, George,' said Chuck urgently. 'I've learned something that means trouble.'

'What's wrong? Isn't the machine behaving?' That was the worst contingency George could imagine. It might delay his return, than which nothing could be more horrible. The way he felt now, even the sight of a TV commercial would seem like manna from heaven. At least it would be some link with home.

'No—it's nothing like that.' Chuck settled himself on the parapet, which was unusual because normally he was scared of the drop. 'I've just found what all this is about.'

'What d'ya mean—I thought we knew.'

'Sure—we know what the monks are trying to do. But we didn't know *why*. It's the craziest thing——'

'Tell me something new,' growled George.

' but old Sam's just come clean with me. You know the way he drops in every afternoon to watch the sheets roll out. Well, this time he seemed rather excited, or at least as near as he'll ever get to it. When I told him that we were on the last cycle he asked me, in that cute English accent of his, if I'd ever wondered what they were trying to do. I said "Sure"—and he told me.'

'Go on: I'll buy it.'

'Well, they believe that when they have listed all His names—and they reckon that there are about nine billion of them—God's purpose will be achieved. The human race will have finished what it was created to do, and there won't be any point in carrying on. Indeed, the very idea is something like blasphemy.'

'Then what do they expect us to do? Commit suicide?'

'There's no need for that. When the list's completed, God steps in and simply winds things up . . . bingo!'

'Oh, I get it. When we finish our job, it will be the end of the world.'

Chuck gave a nervous little laugh.

'That's just what I said to Sam. And do you know what happened? He looked at me in a very queer way, like I'd been stupid in class, and said "It's nothing as trivial as *that*." '

George thought this over for a moment.

'That's what I call taking the Wide View,' he said presently. 'But what d'ya suppose we should do about it? I don't see that it makes the slightest difference to us. After all, we already knew that they were crazy.'

'Yes—but don't you see what may happen? When the list's complete and the Last Trump doesn't blow—or whatever it is they expect—we may get the blame. It's our machine they've been using. I don't like the situation one little bit.'

'I see,' said George slowly. 'You've got a point there. But this sort of thing's happened before, you know. When I was a kid down in Louisiana we had a crackpot preacher who said the world was going to end next Sunday. Hundreds of people believed him—even sold their homes. Yet when nothing happened, they didn't turn nasty as you'd expect. They just decided that he'd made a mistake in his calculations and went right on believing. I guess some of them still do.'

'Well, this isn't Louisiana, in case you hadn't noticed. There are just two of us and hundreds of these monks. I like them, and I'll be sorry for old Sam when his lifework backfires on him. But all the same, I wish I was somewhere else.'

'I've been wishing that for weeks. But there's nothing we can do until the contract's finished and the transport arrives to fly us out.'

'Of course,' said Chuck thoughtfully, 'we could always try a bit of sabotage.'

'Like hell we could! That would make things worse.'

'Not the way I meant. Look at it like this. The machine will finish its run four days from now, on the present twenty-hours-a-day basis. The transport calls in a week. O.K.—then all we need do is to find something that wants replacing during one of the overhaul periods—something that will hold up the works for a couple of days. We'll fix it of course, but not too quickly. If we time matters properly, we can be down at the airfield when the last name pops out of the register. They won't be able to catch us then.'

'I don't like it,' said George. 'It will be the first time I ever walked out on a job. Besides, it would make them suspicious. No. I'll sit tight and take what comes.'

'I *still* don't like it,' he said, seven days later, as the tough little mountain ponies carried them down the winding road. 'And don't you think I'm running away because I'm afraid. I'm just sorry for those poor old guys up there, and I don't want to be around when they find what suckers they've been. Wonder how Sam will take it?'

'It's funny,' replied Chuck, 'but when I said good-bye I got the idea he knew we were walking out on him—and that he didn't care because he knew the machine was running smoothly and that the job would soon be finished. After that—well, of course, for him there just isn't any After That . . .'

George turned in his saddle and stared back up the mountain road. This was the last place from which one could get a clear view of the lamasery. The squat, angular buildings were silhouetted against the afterglow of the sunset: here and there, lights gleamed like portholes in the sides of an ocean liner. Electric lights, of course, sharing the same circuit as the Mark V. How much longer would they share it, wondered George. Would the monks smash up the computer in their rage and disappointment? Or would they just sit down quietly and begin their calculations all over again?

He knew exactly what was happening up on the mountain at this very moment. The High Lama and his assistants would be sitting in their silk robes, inspecting the sheets as the junior monks carried them away from the typewriters and pasted them into the great volumes. No one would be saying anything. The only sound would be the incessant patter, the never-ending rainstorm of the keys hitting the paper, for the Mark V itself was utterly silent as it flashed through its thousands of calculations a second. Three months of this, thought George, was enough to start anyone climbing up the wall.

'There she is!' called Chuck, pointing down into the valley. 'Ain't she beautiful!'

She certainly was, thought George. The battered old DC 3 lay at the end of the runway like a tiny silver cross. In two hours she would be bearing them away to freedom and sanity. It was a thought worth savouring like a fine liqueur. George let it roll round his mind as the pony trudged patiently down the slope.

The swift night of the high Himalayas was now almost upon them. Fortunately the road was very good, as roads went in this region, and they were both carrying torches. There was not the slightest danger, only a certain discomfort from the bitter cold. The sky overhead was perfectly clear and ablaze with the familiar, friendly stars. At least there would be no risk, thought George, of the pilot being unable to take off because of weather conditions. That had been his only remaining worry.

He began to sing, but gave it up after a while. This vast arena of mountains, gleaming like whitely hooded ghosts on every side, did not encourage such ebullience. Presently George glanced at his watch.

'Should be there in an hour,' he called back over his shoulder to Chuck. Then he added, in an afterthought: 'Wonder if the computer's finished its run? It was due about now.'

Chuck didn't reply, so George swung round in his saddle. He could just see Chuck's face, a white oval turned towards the sky.

'Look,' whispered Chuck, and George lifted his eyes to heaven. (There is always a last time for everything.)

Overhead, without any fuss, the stars were going out.

PANEL GAME

BRIAN W. ALDISS

IT WAS Christmas. Snow fell by courtesy of Home-Count
Climatic.

Rick Sheridan came off shift early, flying his helic deftly
through the white clouds, and keeping by long custom
between the altitude levels prescribed for his particular
consumer-class. As far as he might be said to have a character, his character was cheerful. He exhibited this cheer-
fulness now by whistling.

The sound filled the little cockpit, competing with the
bope music issuing from the 3-inch screen telly strapped
on his wrist.

Christmas! It was proverbially the time of festivity and
maximum consumption. It was a period when everyone
would be happy—except, possibly, he warned himself, his
wife, Neata. Her moodiness had become trying of late. The
mere thought of it knocked his whistle off key.

For the difficult business of landing, Rick switched on to
auto. This luxury had been fitted by Happy Hover Ltd.
only two months ago. With the faintest of sighs, the helic
leafed down, below the clouds, below the aerial levels,
below the roof-tops, and squatted in the Sheridan back
garden.

The garden was a large one, as gardens went, ten feet
by sixteen, and covered by neo-concrete. Rick jumped out
and stretched himself. Although he was all of twenty-eight,

183

he suddenly felt young and healthy again. Appetite stirred sluttishly in his stomach.

'Oh for a bowl of tasty, toothable Cob Corners!' he cried exultantly, and bounded for the back door.

He was high enough up the consumer hierarchy to own a magnificent two-room dwelling. Walking through the Disposing room, he entered the Gazing room and called: 'Neata!'

She was sitting quietly at the Relaxtable, laboriously mending a little labour-saving device, her fair head bent in concentration. Her smile of welcome formed easily and naturally round her new teeth, and she jumped up, throwing her arms round him—carefully, so as not to crumple his teddy tie.

'Ricky, darling, you're early!' she exclaimed.

'I hit my quota ahead of schedule,' he explained proudly. 'Thanks to Howlett's.'

Their only child, Goya, jumped up and ran to greet her daddy. She managed to do it backwards, thus keeping her eyes fixed on the wall screens, where Sobold the Soap King was facing three dirty-looking criminals single-handed.

Rick's eyes glistened behind their contact lenses. He reflected how affectionate the child was for a three-year-old, but something in the little girl's actions must have displeased her mother, for Neata said irritably: 'Why don't you welcome your father properly?'

'Wanna see old Sobold slosh the slashers,' Goya said defiantly.

'You're old enough to guess what will happen,' Neata said crossly. 'He'll catch them and make them all wash in that creamy, dreamy lather that only Little Britches Soap provides.'

'Don't get angry with her,' Rick said. 'Remember, it's Christmas.'

He took Goya on his knee, and settled down with her to watch Sobold, his hunger forgotten. The wall-screens filled two walls. Before the end of next year, if he worked as well as he was working now, they might be able to afford a third screen. And one day . . . he blushed with excitement at the thought of being surrounded by an image in quadruplicate on all four walls.

A flicker of interference burst over the bright screens. Rick tutted with annoyance; the terrific technical accomplishment of telly was something upon which every civilized consumer prided himself, but it was nevertheless obvious that just lately there had been more misting than usual on the screens. Rick found himself recalling the rumours, dim and evasive, which he heard while at work; rumours of a vile movement to overthrow the present happy régime, of determined men with new weapons at their command.

Dismissing the idea irritably, he turned full attention on to the screens. Justice and cleanliness having overtaken Sobold's opponents, the next quarter of an hour was to be devoted to 'Mr. Dial's Diary', a comic serial lampooning twentieth-century farm life, presented by the makers of Grinbaum's Meat Bars.

'Time for bed, Goya.' Neata declared, and despite the young lady's protests she was whisked into the Disposing room for an encounter with Little Britches, Ardentifrices and Juxon's ('Nun-better') Drying powder. Rick seized this opportunity while he was alone to spend ten minutes looking into his Pornograph, but his attention was recalled by a jolly announcer in the Grinbaum uniform calling out: 'Well, customers, there we have to leave Mr. Dial for now. Is his prize cow really going to calve? Will Sally Hobkin get that big kiss she deserves? Your guess is as good as mine, suckers. One thing *everybody* is sure about is the goodness, the sheer brothy, spothy goodness, of Grinbaum's Meat Bars. A whole carcass goes into each of those chewy little cubes.'

And then leaning, as it seemed, almost out of the screen. the announcer suddenly bellowed harshly: 'Have you bought *your* quote of Grinbaum's Meat Bars today, Sheridan?'

Cut. Screen blank. Ten seconds till next programme.

'He certainly puts that over well,' Rick gasped proudly, passing a hand over his brow. 'It always makes me jump.'

'It makes me jump too,' said Neata flatly, leading a night-dressed Goya into the room.

This device whereby consumers could be individually named was the latest, and possibly cleverest, accomplishment of telly. The announcer had actually named no names; instead, at the correct moment, a signal transmitted from the studio activated a circuit at the receiving end which, in every individual home, promptly bellowed out the surname of the head consumer of the family.

Neata pressed the Relaxtable, and a section of it sprang into a bed. Goya was put in, and given her cup of steaming, happy-dreaming Howlett's. She had hardly drunk the last mouthful before she sank down on the pillow, yawning.

'Sleep well!' Neata said gently, pressing the child's ear-plugs into place. She felt tired herself, she hardly knew why. It would be a relief when her turn came for Howlett's and Payne's Painless Plugs.

There was no switching the screens off and now that telly provided a twenty-four-hour service, the aids to sleep were a necessity.

'This is Green Star, B channel,' announced the screens. 'The Dewlap Chair Hour! ! !'

'Must we watch this?' Neata asked, as three dancing, screaming nudes burst into view, legs waving, bosoms bouncing.

'We could try Green Star A.'

Green Star A had a play, which had already begun. They tried Green Star C, but that had a travel programme on, and Rick was bored by other countries—and a little afraid of them. They turned back to the Dewlap Hour, and gradually relaxed into semi-mindlessness.

There were three other coloured star systems, each with

three channels at their disposal, theoretically at least. But Green Star was the official consumer system for their consumer-class; obviously it would be wasteful for the Sheridans to watch White Star, which advertised commodities they could not afford, such as shower-purges, stratostruts, tellysolids and bingoproofs.

If they did watch White Star, there was, unfortunately, no guarantee that telly was not watching them. For since the installation of 'wave-bounce', some ten years ago, every wall screen was a reciprocal—which meant, in plain language, that every viewer could be viewed from telly. This innovation was the source of some of the very best programmes, for viewers could sit and watch themselves viewing telly.

Dewlap was showing one of the numerous and ever-popular panel games. Three blindfold men and a blindfold woman were being passed patent custards, cake-mixes and detergents; they had to distinguish between the different commodities by taste alone. A compère in shirt sleeves awarded blows over the head for incorrect guesses.

Just tonight—perhaps because it was Christmas—the sight of Gilbert Lardner having his head tapped failed to enthral Rick. He began to walk about the Gazing room, quite an easy matter since, except for the Relaxtable in which Goya lay drugged, there was a complete absence of furniture.

Catching Neata's curious gaze upon him, Rick moved out into the garden. It was not fair to distract her from her viewing.

The snow still fell, still by courtesy of Home-Count Climatic. He did not feel the cool night air, snug in his Moxon's Mock-wool. Absently, he ran his hand over the helic, its blunt vanes, its atomic motor, its telly suppressor, its wheels. All maintenance, of course, was done by the helic drome: there was nothing he could fiddle with. Indeed, there was nothing he could do at all.

Like a sensible fellow, like all his sensible neighbours—

N

whom he had hardly so much as seen—he went back indoors and sat before the screens.

Five minutes later came the unprecedented knock at the door.

The shortage of arable land in England, acute in the twentieth century, became critical in the twenty-first. Mankind's way of reproducing himself being what it is, the more houses that were erected on the dwindling acres, the more houses were needed. These two problems, which were really but facets of one problem, were solved dramatically and unexpectedly. After telly's twenty-four-hour services were introduced, it was realized by those who had the interests of the nation at heart (a phrase denoting those who were paid from public taxes) that nine-tenths of the people needed neither windows nor friends: telly was all in all to them.

A house without windows can be built in any surroundings. It can be built in rows of hundreds or blocks of thousands. Nor need roads be a hindrance to this agglomeration: an airborne population needs no roads.

A house without friends is freed from ostentation. There is no longer any urge to keep up with the Joneses, or whoever may come in. One needs, in fact, only two rooms: a room in which to watch the screens, and a room in which to store the Meat Bars and other items which the screens hypnotize one into buying.

So telly changed the face of England almost overnight. The Sheridan house, like a great many others, was in the midst of a nest of houses stretching for a mile or more in all directions; it could be reached only by something small enough to alight in the garden.

So for many reasons the knock on the door was very much a surprise.

'Whoever can it *be*?' asked Rick uneasily.

'I don't know,' Neata said. She too had heard rumours

of a subversive movement; a momentary—and not unpleas-
ing—vision attended her of two masked men coming in
and smashing the wall screens. But of course masked men
would not bother to knock.

'Perhaps it's somebody from Grinbaum's Meat Bars,'
suggested Rick. 'I forgot to buy any today.'

'Don't be so silly, Rick,' his wife said impatiently. 'You
know their factory must be purely automatic. Go and *see*
who it is.'

That was something he had not thought of. You had to
hand it to women. . . . He got up and went reluctantly to
open the door, smoothing his hair and his tie on the way.

A solid-looking individual stood in the drifting snow. His
helic was parked against Rick's. He wore some sort of a
cloak over his Mock-wool: obviously, he was of a higher
consumer-class than the Sheridans.

'Er . . .' said Rick.

'May I come in?' asked the stranger in the sort of voice
always hailed on the screens as resonant. 'I'm an escaped
criminal.'

'Er . . .'

'I'm not dangerous. Don't be alarmed.'

'The little girl's in bed,' Rick said, clutching at the first
excuse which entered his head.

'Have no fear,' said the stranger, still resonantly; 'kid-
napping is not one of the numerous offences on my crime
sheet.'

He swept magnificently past Rick, through the dark Disposing room and into the Gazer. Neata jumped up as he
entered. He bowed low and pulled the cloak from his
shoulders with an eloquent gesture which scattered snow
over the room.

'Madam, forgive my intrusion,' he said, the organ note
more noticeable than ever. 'I throw myself upon your
mercy.'

'Ooh, you talk like someone on a panel game,' Neata
gasped.

'I thank you for that from the bottom of my heart,' said the stranger, and announced himself as Black Jack Gabriel.

Rick hardly heard. He was taking in the thick-set figure in its smart attire, and the curiously impressive streak of white hair on the leonine head (the fellow must be thirty if he was a day). He also took in the meaningful way Neata and Black Jack were looking at each other.

'I'm Neata Sheridan, and this is my husband, Rick,' Neata was saying.

'A delightful name,' said Black Jack, bowing at Rick and grinning ingratiatingly.

'It's only short for Rickmansworth,' said Neata, a little acidly.

Black Jack, standing facing but entirely ignoring the screens, began to speak. He was a born elocutionist, and soon even Rick ceased to blush—a nervous habit which manifested itself on the rare occasions when he was face to face with a real human being.

Black Jack had a dramatic tale to tell of his capture by armed police, who had chased him across roofs thirty storeys above ground level. For the last nine years he had been imprisoned in Holloway, condemned to hard labour, knitting hemp mittens for the cameramen of Outside Telly.

Suddenly, only a few hours ago, an opportunity for escape had presented itself. Black Jack had broken into the Governor's suite, exchanged clothes, and flown off in the Governor's helic.

'And here I am,' he said. 'I just landed at random—and how lucky I was to find you two.'

Despite some opposition from an outbreak of bope music from the screen, Rick had been listening with great attention.

'If it's not a rude question, Mr. Black,' he said, 'what did you do wrong?'

'That's rather a long story,' Black Jack said modestly,

knitting his eyebrows but positively smiling at Neata. 'You see, England used to be rather a strange place. In those days—you must have seen so much entertainment you would not remember—there was a government. There were also several industries, and something known as "free enterprise" flourishing. The government used to "nationalize" (as they called it) any industry which looked like getting too big and prosperous.

'Well, one of these industries was called Television—telly is the modern term. It was getting so big, the government took it over, but it was so big, it took over the government. A case of the tail wagging the dog, you see.

'Soon, everything was telly. And perpetual entertainment did a lot of good. Now half the people in the country work —directly or indirectly—for telly. It did away with unemployment, over-employment, strikes, neuroses, wars, housing problems, crime and football pools. Perpetual entertainment was here to stay.'

'You tell it so well,' Neata said. She was virtually cuddling against him. 'But what did you do to earn your long prison sentence?'

'I was the last Prime Minister,' Black Jack said. 'I voted against perpetual entertainment.'

Neata gasped.

So did Rick. Drawing himself up, he said : 'Then we don't want any of your sort in our house. I must ask you to leave before the H. Brogan's Watches' show comes on.'

'Oh, don't make him go,' pleaded Neata. She suddenly realized that here was the calibre of man she had been waiting for. He might well be leader of the rumoured subversive movement : he might cause interference on every wall screen in the country : but she could forgive no applaud!—everything, if he would just roll his eyes again.

'I said "Go",' demanded Rick.

'I had no intention of staying,' said Black Jack coolly. 'I'm on my way to Bali or Spain or India or somewhere without perpetual entertainment.'

'Then what did you come here for in the first place?'
Rick asked.

'Merely to borrow some food to sustain me on my journey. The Governor's helic happened not to be provisioned
for a long flight. Surely you'll do that for me?'

'Of course we will—if you must go,' said Neata.

'Why should we?' asked Rick. 'I'll be a Dutchman if I
lift a finger to help a criminal.' But catching sight of his
wife's clenched fists and suddenly blazing eyes, he muttered
miserably: 'O.K., call me Hans,' and made off into the
Disposing room.

Ardently, the self-confessed Prime Minister turned to
Neata. 'How can I ever thank you for your assistance,
madam,' he breathed. 'It will be useless for you to forget
me, for I shall never forget you!'

'Nor I you,' she said. 'I think—oh . . . I think you're
wonderful, and—and I *hate* the telly.'

With swimming eyes, she peered up at him. He was
pressing her hand: *he* was pressing *her* hand. It was the
most wonderful moment of her life; her heart told her she
was closer to the Meaning of Existence than she had ever
been. Now he was leaning towards her—and Rick was
back in the room again.

Hardly daring to leave them alone, he had snatched up
a bag of dried prunes, two cartons of Silvery Soggmash,
a cake, a sackful of Dehydratede Olde Englishe Fishe and
Chyps ('There's no food like an old food') and a tin of
Grinbaums which had been previously overlooked.

'Here you are,' he said ungraciously. 'Now go.'

Black Jack was meekness itself, now his object had been
gained. He seemed, indeed, pleased to be off, Neata thought
dejectedly; but doubtless such police as could be spared
from viewing would be on his trail, and he could not afford
to delay.

Rick followed the intruder out into the snow, which was
still falling by courtesy of H-C.C. Black Jack flung the
provisions into the boot of his helic and jumped gracefully

into the driver's seat. He raised a hand in ironical salute and called: 'Happy Christmas!' The helic lifted.

'Good-bye!' Neata called romantically and then, more romantically still: *'Bon Voyage!'*

But already the machine was lost in the whirling white flakes.

'Come on in,' Rick grunted.

They exchanged no words indoors. Morosely, Rick glared at the wall screens. Somehow, now, the savour was gone. Even the H. Brogan's Watches' Show had lost its appeal. He got up and paced about restlessly, fiddling with his teddy tie.

'Oh heck,' he said. 'Let's try White Star. I don't suppose any supervisors are watching us. We need a change, that's what.'

He flicked the controls over to White Star A, and gasped in astonishment. Neata gasped too, a little more gustily.

A sumptuous lounge showed on the screens. An immaculate announcer and three immaculate guests were leaning back in their chairs to watch a figure enter a door and approach the camera.

The figure, in its swagger cloak, with the distinguished streak of white in its hair, was unmistakable. It bowed to the unseen audience.

Nervously, a little over-heartily, the announcer was saying: 'Well, consumers, here comes the scallywag of the Bryson Brainbath Hour, safe back in the studio.' And turning to the newcomer he said: 'Well, Gervaise McByron—alias Black Jack Gabriel—your forfeit in this special Christmas edition of our popular panel game, "Fifty Queries", in which you got lowest score, was to go out and talk your way into a green consumer-class home, returning with a souvenir of your visit. You've certainly carried out instructions to the letter!'

Popular White telly-star McByron smiled lavishly, said: 'I did my best!' and deposited some prunes, some Soggy-

mash, a cake, Fishe and Chyps and a tin of Grinbaums at
the announcer's feet.

'Your patter was terribly convincing,' said the announcer
uneasily. 'I just hope none of our viewers believed a word
you said about—er, Big Mother Telly. I almost believed
you myself, ha, ha!'

'You'll get suspended for this, McByron,' opined a decorative lady who had been included on the panel for the
sake of her undulating façade. 'You went too far. Far too
far.'

'We watched every moment of your performance in the
Sheridan shack via wave-bounce reciprocal,' said the announcer. 'I just hope none of our viewers believed a
word——'

'Tell me, McByron,' cut in the decorative woman coldly,
'what did you really think of Mrs. Sheridan?'

'If you want a frank answer,' began McByron bluntly,
'compared with you, Lady Patricia So-and-so Burton, she
was an absolute——'

'And so ends this special Christmas edition of "Fifty
Queries",' cried the announcer frantically, jumping up and
waving his hands. 'It was brought to you by courtesy of
Bryson's Brainbaths. Don't forget: a mind that thinks
is a mind that stinks. Good night, consumers, everywhere.'

Cut. Screen black. Ten seconds to next programme.

Slowly, Rick turned to face his wife.

'There!' he said. 'Disgraced! That—that trickster! We
were just a spot of amusement on a snob-class panel show.
Now are you ashamed?'

'Don't say anything, please, Rick,' Neata said distantly.
There was something so commanding in her tone that her
husband turned away and abjectly switched back to Green
Star.

Neata walked pensively out of the room. She still
clutched the wicked little device which McByron, alias
Black Jack, had pressed into her hand. Then, it had been

startlingly cold; now, her palm had made it hot. She knew
what it was, she knew what she had to do with it.

'Deadly . . .' she whispered to herself. 'Deadly. . . .
The end of civilization as we know it.'

The metal was a challenge in her grasp.

Ah, but McByron was clever! She was dizzy at his impudence. Although evidently a leading tellystar, he was
nevertheless a saboteur, a member—perhaps the leader!—
of the subversives. And he had dared to pass on this weapon
and to deliver his inspiring message of doubt in front of
thousands of viewers.

'What a man!'

Neata was out in the snow now. She looked with strained
face at the little device. It had to be fitted on to Rick's
helic. Poor Rick—but he would never know! The thought
that she was helping in a mighty, silent revolution lent her
determination.

Quickly, she bent down and fitted the anti-telly suppressor into Rick's helic.

THE MAN IN ASBESTOS: AN ALLEGORY OF THE FUTURE

STEPHEN LEACOCK

TO BEGIN with let me admit that I did it on purpose. Perhaps it was partly from jealousy.

It seemed unfair that other writers should be able at will to drop into a sleep of four or five hundred years, and to plunge head first into a distant future and be a witness of its marvels.

I wanted to do that too.

I always had been, I still am, a passionate student of social problems. The world of today with its roaring machinery, the unceasing toil of its working classes, its strife, its poverty, its wars, its cruelty, appals me as I look at it. I love to think of the time that must come some day when man will have conquered nature, and the toil-worn human race enter upon an era of peace.

I loved to think of it, and I longed to see it.

So I set about the thing deliberately.

What I wanted to do was to fall asleep after the customary fashion, for two or three hundred years at least, and wake and find myself in the marvel world of the future.

I made my preparations for the sleep.

I bought all the comic papers that I could find, even the illustrated ones. I carried them up to my room in my hotel; with them I brought up a pork pie and dozens and dozens of doughnuts. I ate the pie and the doughnuts, then sat back in the bed and read the comic papers one after the other. Finally, as I felt the awful lethargy stealing upon me, I reached out my hand for the *London Weekly Times*, and held up the editorial page before my eyes.

It was, in a way, clear, straight suicide, but I did it.

I could feel my senses leaving me. In the room across the hall there was a man singing. His voice, that had been loud, came fainter and fainter through the transom. I fell into a sleep, the deep immeasurable sleep in which the very existence of the outer world was hushed. Dimly I could feel the days go past, then the years, and then the long passage of the centuries.

Then, not as is were gradually, but quite suddenly, I woke up, sat up, and looked about me.

Where was I?

Well might I ask myself.

I found myself lying, or rather sitting up, on a broad couch. I was in a great room, dim, gloomy, and dilapidated in its general appearance, and apparently, from its glass cases and the stuffed figures that they contained, some kind of museum.

Beside me sat a man. His face was hairless, but neither old nor young. He wore clothes that looked like the grey ashes of paper that had burned and kept its shape. He was looking at me quietly, but with no particular surprise or interest.

'Quick,' I said, eager to begin; 'where am I? Who are you? What year is this; is it the year 3000, or what is it?'

He drew in his breath with a look of annoyance on his face.

'What a queer, excited way you have of speaking,' he said.

'Tell me,' I said again, 'is this the year 3000?'

'I think I know what you mean,' he said; 'but really I haven't the faintest idea. I should think it must be at least that, within a hundred years or so; but nobody has kept track of them for so long, it's hard to say.'

'Don't you keep track of them any more?' I gasped.

'We used to,' said the man. 'I myself can remember that a century or two ago there were still a number of people who used to try to keep track of the year, but it died out along with so many other faddish things of that kind. Why,' he continued, showing for the first time a sort of animation in his talk, 'what was the use of it? You see, after we eliminated death——'

'Eliminated death!' I cried, sitting upright. 'Good God!'

'What was that expression you used?' queried the man.

'Good God!' I repeated.

'Ah,' he said, 'never heard it before. But I was saying that after we had eliminated Death, and Food, and Change, we had practically got rid of Events, and——'

'Stop!' I said, my brain reeling. 'Tell me one thing at a time.'

'Humph!' he ejaculated. 'I see, you must have been asleep a long time. Go on then and ask questions. Only, if you don't mind, just as few as possible, and please don't get interested or excited.'

Oddly enough the first question that sprang to my lips was——

'What are those clothes made of?'

'Asbestos,' answered the man. 'They last hundreds of years. We have one suit each, and there are billions of them piled up, if anybody wants a new one.'

'Thank you,' I answered. 'Now tell me where I am?'

'You are in a museum. The figures in the cases are specimens like yourself. But here,' he said, 'if you want really to find out about what is evidently a new epoch to you, get off your platform and come out on Broadway and sit on a bench.'

I got down.

As we passed through the dim and dust-covered buildings I looked curiously at the figures in the cases.

'By Jove!' I said, looking at one figure in blue clothes with a belt and baton, 'that's a policeman!'

'Really,' said my new acquaintance, 'is *that* what a *policeman* was? I've often wondered. What used they to be used for?'

'Used for!' I repeated in perplexity. 'Why, they stood at the corner of the street.'

'Ah, yes, I see,' he said, 'so as to shoot at the people. You must excuse my ignorance,' he continued, 'as to some of your social customs in the past. When I took my education I was operated upon for social history, but the stuff they used was very inferior.'

I didn't in the least understand what the man meant, but had no time to question him, for at that moment we came out upon the street, and I stood riveted in astonishment.

Broadway! Was it possible? The change was absolutely appalling! In place of the roaring thoroughfare that I had known, this silent, moss-grown desolation. Great buildings fallen into ruin through the sheer stress of centuries of wind and weather, the sides of them coated over with a growth of fungus and moss! The place was soundless. Not a vehicle moved. There were no wires overhead—no sound of life or movement except, here and there, there passed slowly to and fro human figures dressed in the same asbestos clothes as my acquaintance, with the same hairless faces, and the same look of infinite age upon them.

Good heavens! And was this the era of the Conquest that I had hoped to see! I had always taken for granted, I do not know why, that humanity was destined to move forward. This picture of what seemed desolation on the ruins of our civilization rendered me almost speechless.

There were little benches placed here and there on the street. We sat down.

'Improved, isn't it,' said the man in asbestos, 'since the days when you remember it?'

He seemed to speak quite proudly.

I gasped out a question.

'Where are the street cars and the motors?'

'Oh, done away with long ago,' he said; 'how awful they must have been. The noise of them!' and his asbestos clothes rustled with a shudder.

'But how do you get about?'

'We don't,' he answered. 'Why should we? It's just the same being here as being anywhere else.' He looked at me with an infinity of dreariness in his face.

A thousand questions surged into my mind at once. I asked one of the simplest.

'But how do you get back and forwards to your work?'

'Work!' he said. 'There isn't any work. It's finished. The last of it was all done centuries ago.'

I looked at him a moment open mouthed. Then I turned and looked again at the grey desolation of the street with the asbestos figures moving here and there.

I tried to pull my senses together. I realized that if I was to unravel this new and undreamed-of future, I must go at it systematically and step by step.

'I see,' I said after a pause, 'that momentous things have happened since my time. I wish you would let me ask you about it all systematically, and would explain it to me bit by bit. First, what do you mean by saying that there is no work?'

'Why,' answered my strange acquaintance, 'it died out of itself. Machinery killed it. If I remember rightly, you had a certain amount of machinery even in your time. You had done very well with steam, made a good beginning with electricity, though I think radio energy had hardly as yet been put to use.'

I nodded assent.

'But you found it did you no good. The better your machines, the harder you worked. The more things you had the more you wanted. The pace of life grew swifter and swifter. You cried out, but it would not stop. You were all caught in the cogs of your own machine. None of you could see the end.'

'That is quite true,' I said. 'How do you know it all?'

'Oh,' answered the Man in Asbestos, 'that part of my education was very well operated—I see you do not know what I mean. Never mind, I can tell you that later. Well, then, there came, probably almost two hundred years after your time, the Era of the Great Conquest of Nature, the final victory of Man and Machinery.'

'They did conquer it?' I asked quickly, with a thrill of the old hope in my veins again.

'Conquered it,' he said, 'beat it out! Fought it to a stand-still! Things came one by one, then faster and faster, in a hundred years it was all done. In fact, just as soon as mankind turned its energy to decreasing its needs instead of increasing its desires, the whole thing was easy. Chemical Food came first. Heavens! The simplicity of it. And in your time thousands of millions of people tilled and grub-bed at the soil from morning till night. I've seen specimens of them—farmers, they called them. There's one in the museum. After the invention of Chemical Food we piled up enough in the emporiums in a year to last for centuries. Agriculture went overboard. Eating and all that goes with it, domestic labour, housework—all ended. Nowadays one takes a concentrated pill every year or so, that's all. The whole digestive apparatus, as you knew it, was a clumsy thing that had been bloated up like a set of bagpipes through the evolution of its use!'

I could not forbear to interrupt. 'Have you and these people,' I said, 'no stomachs—no apparatus?'

'Of course we have,' he answered, 'but we use it to some purpose. Mine is largely filled with my education—but there! I am anticipating again. Better let me go on as I was. Chemical Food came first; that cut off almost one-third of the work, and then came Asbestos Clothes. That was wonderful! In one year humanity made enough suits to last for ever and ever. That, of course, could never have been if it hadn't been connected with the revolt of women and the fall of Fashion.'

'Have the Fashions gone,' I asked, 'that insane, extravagant idea of——' I was about to launch into one of my old-time harangues about the sheer vanity of decorative dress, when my eye rested on the moving figures in asbestos, and I stopped.

'All gone,' said the Man in Asbestos. 'Then next to that we killed, or practically killed, the changes of climate. I don't think that in your day you properly understood how much of your work was due to the shifts of what you called the weather. It meant the need of all kinds of special clothes and houses and shelters, a wilderness of work. How dreadful it must have been in your day—wind and storms, great wet masses—what did you call them?—clouds—flying through the air, the ocean full of salt, was it not?—tossed and torn by the wind, snow thrown all over everything, hail, rain—how awful!'

'Sometimes,' I said, 'it was very beautiful. But how did you alter it?'

'Killed the weather!' answered the Man in Asbestos. 'Simple as anything—turned its forces loose one against the other, altered the composition of the sea so that the top became all more or less gelatinous. I really can't explain it, as it is an operation that I never took at school, but it made the sky grey, as you see it, and the sea gum-coloured, the weather all the same. It cut out fuel and houses and an infinity of work with them!'

He paused a moment. I began to realize something of the course of evolution that had happened.

'So,' I said, 'the conquest of nature meant that presently there was no more work to do?'

'Exactly,' he said, 'nothing left.'

'Food enough for all?'

'Too much,' he answered.

'Houses and clothes?'

'All you like,' said the Man in Asbestos, waving his hand. 'There they are. Go out and take them. Of course, they're falling down—slowly, very slowly. But they'll last for centuries yet, nobody need bother.'

Then I realized, I think for the first time, just what work had meant in the old life, and how much of the texture of life itself had been bound up in the keen effort of it.

Presently my eyes looked upward: dangling at the top of a moss-grown building I saw what seemed to be the remains of telephone wires.

'What became of all that,' I said, 'the telegraph and the telephone and all the system of communication?'

'Ah,' said the Man in Asbestos, 'that was what a telephone meant, was it? I knew that it had been suppressed centuries ago. Just what was it for?'

'Why,' I said with enthusiasm, 'by means of the telephone we could talk to anybody, call up anybody, and talk at any distance.'

'And anybody could call you up at any time and talk?' said the Man in Asbestos, with something like horror. 'How awful! What a dreadful age yours was, to be sure. No, the telephone and all the rest of it, all the transportation and intercommunication was cut out and forbidden. There was no sense in it. You see,' he added, 'what you don't realize is that people after your day became gradually more and more reasonable. Take the railroad, what good was that? It brought into every town a lot of people from every other town. Who wanted them? Nobody. When work stopped and commerce ended, and food was needless, and the weather killed, it was foolish to move about. So it was all terminated. Anyway,' he said, with a quick look of apprehension and a change in his voice, 'it was dangerous!'

'So!' I said. 'Dangerous! You still have danger?'

'Why, yes,' he said, 'there's always the danger of getting broken.'

'What do you mean?' I asked.

'Why,' said the Man in Asbestos, 'I suppose it's what you would call being dead. Of course, in one sense there's been no death for centuries past; we cut that out. Disease and death were simply a matter of germs. We found them one

o

by one. I think that even in your day you had found one
or two of the easier, the bigger ones?'

I nodded.

'Yes, you had found diphtheria and typhoid, and, if I am
right, there were some outstanding, like scarlet fever and
smallpox, that you called ultra-microscopic, and which
you were still hunting for, and others that you didn't even
suspect. Well, we hunted them down one by one and destroyed them. Strange that it never occurred to any of you
that Old Age was only a germ! It turned out to be quite
a simple one, but it was so distributed in its action that
you never even thought of it.'

'And you mean to say,' I ejaculated in amazement, looking at the Man in Asbestos, 'that nowadays you live for
ever?'

'I wish,' he said, 'that you hadn't that peculiar, excitable
way of talking; you speak as if everything *mattered* so tremendously. Yes,' he continued, 'we live for ever, unless, of
course, we get broken. That happens sometimes. I mean
that we may fall over a high place or bump on something, and snap ourselves. You see, we're just a little brittle
still—some remnant, I suppose, of the Old Age germ—and
we have to be careful. In fact,' he continued, 'I don't mind
saying that accidents of this sort were the most distress-
ing feature of our civilization till we took steps to cut out
all accidents. We forbid all street cars, street traffic, aero-
planes, and so on. The risks of your time,' he said, with a
shiver of his asbestos clothes, 'must have been awful.'

'They were,' I answered, with a new kind of pride in
my generation that I had never felt before, 'but we thought
it part of the duty of brave people to——'

'Yes, yes,' said the Man in Asbestos impatiently, 'please
don't get excited. I know what you mean. It was quite
irrational.'

We sat silent for a long time. I looked about me at the
crumbling buildings, the monotone, unchanging sky, and the
dreary, empty street. Here, then, was the fruit of the Con-

quest, here was the elimination of work, the end of hunger and of cold, the cessation of the hard struggle, the downfall of change and death—nay, the very millennium of happiness. And yet, somehow, there seemed something wrong with it all. I pondered, then I put two or three rapid questions, hardly waiting to reflect upon the answers.

'Is there any war now?'

'Done with centuries ago. They took to settling international disputes with a slot machine. After that all foreign dealings were given up. Why have them? Everybody thinks foreigners awful.'

'Are there any newspapers now?'

'Newspapers! What on earth would we want them for? If we should need them at any time there are thousands of old ones piled up. But what is in them, anyway; only things that *happen*, wars and accidents and work and death. When these went newspapers went too. Listen,' continued the Man in Asbestos, 'you seem to have been something of a social reformer, and yet you don't understand the new life at all. You don't understand how completely all our burdens have disappeared. Look at it this way. How used your people to spend all the early part of their lives?'

'Why,' I said, 'our first fifteen years or so were spent in getting education.'

'Exactly,' he answered; 'now notice how we improved on all that. Education in our day is done by surgery. Strange that in your time nobody realized that education was simply a surgical operation. You hadn't the sense to see that what you really did was to slowly remodel, curve and convolute the inside of the brain by a long and painful mental operation. Everything learned was reproduced in a physical difference to the brain. You knew that, but you didn't see the full consequences. Then came the invention of surgical education—the simple system of opening the side of the skull and engrafting into it a piece of prepared brain. At first, of course, they had to use, I suppose, the brains of dead people, and that was ghastly'—here the Man in Asbestos shuddered like a leaf—'but very soon they found how to make moulds that did just as well. After that it was a mere nothing; an operation of a few minutes would suffice to let in poetry or foreign languages or history or anything else that one cared to have. Here, for instance,' he added, pushing back the hair at the side of his head and showing a scar beneath it, 'is the mark where I had my spherical trigonometry let in. That was, I admit, rather painful, but other things, such as English poetry or history, can be inserted absolutely without the least suffering. When I think of your painful, barbarous methods of education through the ear, I shudder at it. Oddly enough, we have found lately that for a great many things there is no need to use the head. We lodge them—things like philosophy and metaphysics, and so on—in what used to be the digestive apparatus. They fill it admirably.'

He paused a moment. Then went on :

'Well, then, to continue, what used to occupy your time and effort after your education?'

'Why,' I said, 'one had, of course, to work, and then, to tell the truth, a great part of one's time and feeling was devoted towards the other sex, towards falling in love and finding some woman to share one's life.'

'Ah,' said the Man in Asbestos, with real interest. 'I've heard about your arrangements with the women, but never quite understood them. Tell me; you say you selected some woman?'

'Yes.'

'And she became what you called your wife?'

'Yes, of course.'

'And you worked for her?' asked the Man in Asbestos in astonishment.

'Yes.'

'And she did not work?'

'No,' I answered, 'of course not.'

'And half of what you had was hers?'

'Yes.'

'And she had the right to live in your house and use your things?'

'Of course,' I answered.

'How dreadful!' said the Man in Asbestos. 'I hadn't realized the horrors of your age till now.'

He sat shivering slightly, with the same timid look in his face as before.

Then it suddenly struck me that of the figures on the street, all had looked alike.

'Tell me,' I said, 'are there no women now? Are they gone too?'

'Oh, no,' answered the Man in Asbestos, 'they're here just the same. Some of those are women. Only, you see, every-thing has been changed now. It all came as part of their great revolt, their desire to be like the men. Had that begun in your time?'

'Only a little,' I answered; 'they were beginning to ask for votes and equality.'

'That's it,' said my acquaintance, 'I couldn't think of the word. Your women, I believe, were something awful, were they not? Covered with feathers and skins and dazzling colours made of dead things all over them? And they laughed, did they not, and had foolish teeth, and at any moment they could inveigle you into one of those con-tracts! Ugh!'

He shuddered.

'Asbestos,' I said (I knew no other name to call him), as I turned on him in wrath, 'Asbestos, do you think that those jelly-bag Equalities out on the street there, with their ash-barrel suits, can be compared for one moment with our unredeemed, unreformed, heaven-created, hobble-skirted women of the twentieth century?'

Then, suddenly, another thought flashed into my mind——

'The children,' I said, 'where are the children? Are there any?'

'Children,' he said, 'no! I have never heard of there being any such things for at least a century. Horrible little hobgoblins they must have been! Great big faces, and cried constantly! And *grew*, did they not? Like funguses! I believe they were longer each year than they had been the last, and——'

I rose.

'Asbestos!' I said, 'this, then, is your coming Civilization, your millennium. This dull, dead thing, with the work and the burden gone out of life, and with them all the joy and the sweetness of it. For the old struggle—mere stagnation, and in place of danger and death, the dull monotony of security and the horror of an unending decay! Give me back,' I cried, and I flung wide my arms to the dull air, 'the old life of danger and stress, with its hard toil and its bitter chances, and its heartbreaks. I see its value! I know its worth! Give me no rest,' I cried aloud——

'Yes, but give a rest to the rest of the corridor!' cried an angered voice that broke in upon my exultation.

Suddenly my sleep had gone.

I was back again in the room of my hotel, with the hum of the wicked, busy old world all about me, and loud in my ears the voice of the indignant man across the corridor.

'Quit your blatting, you infernal blatherskite,' he was calling. 'Come down to earth.'

I came.

GLOSSARY

This short glossary of SF terms is not by any means exhaustive, even though it explains some expressions which do not appear in this anthology.

SPACE

Asteroid belt: a belt of small bodies, often referred to as minor planets, which are in orbit round the sun between Mars and Jupiter. There has been plenty of speculation as to how they got there—a favourite SF solution to the problem is that a planet was disintegrated either in the course of an interstellar war, or by the uncontrolled scientific advances of its own inhabitants.

Corona: a luminous shell of hot gases surrounding the sun and flaring out in wings and streamers. Because of the atmosphere, it can seldom be seen from Earth; but it would be one of the 'beauties' of space travel.

Cosmology: the science of the Universe as a whole.

Dimensions: we live in a three-dimensional world where objects have length, breadth and height. They also exist continuously in time, and from this fact we derive the term 'space-time continuum.'

Galaxy: a star cluster, or stellar system, itself thousands of light-years across. The galaxy to which our solar system belongs is disc-shaped, about 30,000 light-years across, and from 2,000-5,000 light-years thick. We call it 'The Milky Way.' Other galaxies are so far away that even through the 200-inch telescope at Mt. Palomar, they look like mere spirals of gas. These are called spiral-nebulæ; one of the most famous, Andromeda, is about 1,500,000 light-years away.

Light-year: the distance travelled by light in one year at a speed of 186,000 miles per second.

Meteorites: bits of solid matter (nobody is quite sure where they come from) which bombard the Earth's atmosphere. Some of these are smaller than a pin-head, others large enough to reach Earth and make a sizeable crater before they burn out. They would constitute a menace, though not a serious one, to space ships of the future.

Planet: a heavenly body which circles in an elliptical orbit round a star.

Solar system: a sun with all the secondary bodies which circle round it, *e.g.* planets, meteor swarms, comets. Ours is made up of the Sun, Mercury, Venus, Earth, Mars, Asteroids, Jupiter, Saturn, Uranus, Neptune and Pluto, together with numerous meteor swarms and comets. There are millions of solar systems in each galaxy.

Star: a heavenly body which shines with its own light; some, like our sun, have planets circling round them.

Supernova: a star which suddenly explodes into extreme brightness and then dies down again. The first recorded example in modern times was the Nova Cassiopeiæ which appeared in 1572 and was clearly visible as a star at midday.

Universe: the whole of creation known to us. Modern telescopes which can pierce billions of light-years into space, have shown us that the Universe consists of countless galaxies of stars. You will have already noted that galactic distances are so vast that mere figures, like 5,000 light-years, are hardly meaningful to the human mind. The galaxies themselves are, however, grouped together and even greater areas of empty space then separate each group of galaxies from the next. The galaxies and the solar systems of which they consist are not static but are moving through space at great speed. The Universe seems to be expanding, although this is not apparent within a single galaxy or solar system, since these are held together by their own ordinary gravitation. Groups of objects, such as star clusters or associated galaxies, have to be about ten million light-years apart before the expansion-velocity is observable.

SPACE SHIPS

Antigravity: a yet undiscovered principle, or substance, which would eliminate the effects of gravity and so allow a space ship to escape from Earth.

Blast-off: moment of firing a rocket into outer space.

Escape velocity: the speed required to project an object away from the gravitational pull of a heavenly body. For Earth, this is about 25,000 m.p.h.

Hydroponics: the science of growing plants in chemical solutions without soil. Since plants exhale oxygen, a hydroponic tank would both provide food for and replenish the oxygen used by travellers in a space ship.

Hyper-space: even travelling at the speed of light, space travel beyond the solar system is unfeasible. If, however, we could rise above the laws which govern the normal space-time continuum, and travel faster than light, these horizons would be widened. A ship travelling in hyper-space would accelerate to the speed of light, disappear through the 'light-barrier' and appear again near its destination.

Ion-drive: present rocket fuels are heavy and uneconomical, allowing only a poor pay-load. Atomic motors have been an SF dream for many years. The ion-drive is a by-no-means impossible motor which, powered either by solar energy or nuclear power, would fire out ionized gases at great speed.

Orbital-velocity: any speed which will 'balance' gravity and allow an object to continue indefinitely on an elliptical path (orbit) round a heavenly body. The speed depends to some extent on the distance from the body, *e.g.* the first Russian and American Earth satellites were in orbit at about 18,000 m.p.h. several hundred miles up.

Rocket ship: a space ship which depends on the principle of 'action and reaction' for its motive power. The explosion of the rocket fuel, fired backwards, drives the ship forwards. As the explosion is caused by fuel carried by the rocket itself, and as there is no propellor needing an atmosphere before it can produce thrust, the motor will work with maximum efficiency in a vacuum.

Star ship: a vast space ship which carries enough fuel and equipment to transport its passengers and crew beyond the limits of our solar system into the Galaxy.

SOME SF CONVENTIONS

Alien: an intelligent, but inhuman inhabitant of another world.

Android: a robot, or automaton, so skilfully designed as to appear quite human at first sight.

Esp-men, pyscho-police: secret agents who are concerned with ideas and opinions as well as actions—like the 'thought police' in Orwell's 1984

Humanoid: aliens who have evolved into a physical shape similar to that of a human being.

Mutants: members of a species so affected either by atomic radiation or by processes of natural selection, that they are abnormal in some way—either deformed or possessing different characteristics from the rest of their kind.

Pseudo man: similar to an android but an 'organic' or biochemical imitation capable of independent thought.

Telepathy: a mutation favoured by the SF writer is the development of a race of 'mind-readers' who no longer need spoken language to communicate their ideas and emotions.

FURTHER READING

AUTHORS

The following writers are well-known exponents of SF. Their books, many of which will be found in good Public Libraries, are interesting, though not always easy reading.

Nineteenth Century

A. Conan Doyle
Jules Verne
H. G. Wells

Modern

ENGLISH	AMERICAN
Brian W. Aldiss	Isaac Asimov
John Christopher	James Blish
Arthur C. Clarke	Ray Bradbury
C. S. Lewis	Robert Heinlein
Olaf Stapledon	Clifford Simak
John Wyndham	William Tenn
	A. E. Van Vogt

BOOKS

The only short stories included in this list are examples of *Humour*, since this is a theme which can seldom successfully sustain a full-length novel. There are, however, several 'long' short stories. Items for which no publisher is given are stories of this kind, and most of them appear in the anthologies of which a separate list is given.

Certain of these books are also available in paper-back editions.

SPACE

B. W. Aldiss *Non-Stop* Faber & Faber
R. Heinlein *Starman Jones* Sidgwick & Jackson
D. Lindsay *Voyage to Arcturus* Gollancz
J. Verne *From Earth to Moon* Collins
           Round the Moon **Collins**
H. G. Wells *First Men in the Moon* Collins

TIME AND THE FOURTH DIMENSION

B. W. Aldiss *Smoof*
D. Duncan *Occam's Razor* Gollancz
W. Moore *Bring the Jubilee* Heinemann
H. G. Wells *The Time Machine* Heinemann

INVASION

A. C. Clarke *Childhood's End* Sidgwick & Jackson
E. F. Russell *A Present from Joe*
H. G. Wells *The War of the Worlds* Heinemann
J. Wyndham *The Kraken Wakes* Michael Joseph

OTHER WORLDS

J. Blish *Earthman Come Home* Faber & Faber
          They Shall Have Stars Faber & Faber
          A Case of Conscience
R. Bradbury *The Silver Locusts* Hart-Davis
A. C. Clarke *Earthlight* Muller
C. S. Lewis *Out of the Silent Planet* Bodley Head
             Perelandra Bodley Head
M. Shaara *Grenville's Planet*

REALISM

A. C. Clarke *Prelude to Space* Sidgwick & Jackson
             The Sands of Mars Sidgwick & Jackson
             Thirty Seconds Thirty Days

W. GAIL *By Rocket to the Moon* Dodd, Mead & Co.,
   New York
R. HAMILTON *What's It Like Up There?*
R. HEINLEIN *Blowups Happen*

WAR

J. BOLAND *White August* Michael Joseph
J. CHRISTOPHER *The Year of the Comet* Michael Joseph
C. S. LEWIS *That Hideous Strength* Bodley Head
H. G. WELLS *The Shape of Things to Come* Collins

CATASTROPHE

J. CHRISTOPHER *The Death of Grass* Michael Joseph
F. HOYLE *The Black Cloud* Heinemann
H. G. WELLS *The Food of the Gods* Collins
                In the Days of the Comet Collins
J. WYNDHAM *The Chrysalids* Michael Joseph
                The Day of the Triffids Michael Joseph

THE WORLD OF TOMORROW

R. BRADBURY *Farenheit 451* Hart-Davis
A. C. CLARKE *The City and the Stars* Sidgwick & Jackson
A. HUXLEY *Brave New World* Chatto & Windus
G. ORWELL *1984* Secker & Warburg
O. STAPLEDON *Last and First Men* Methuen

HUMOUR

B. W. ALDISS *The Shubshub Race*
R. BRADBURY *The Murderer*
M. ST. CLAIR *Prott*
J. WYNDHAM *Una*

SHORT STORY ANTHOLOGIES

B. W. ALDISS *Space, Time and Nathaniel* Faber & Faber

R. BRADBURY *The Golden Apples of the Sun* Hart-Davis
The Illustrated Man Hart-Davis
ed. E. CRISPIN *Best SF* Faber & Faber
Best SF Two Faber & Faber
Best SF Three Faber & Faber
ed. S. MINES *Startling Stories* Cassell
C. SIMAK *Strangers in the Universe* Weidenfeld & Nicolson
W. TENN *Of All Possible Worlds* Michael Joseph
H. G. WELLS *Collected Stories* Collins

GENERAL SCIENTIFIC READING

A. C. CLARKE *The Young Traveller in Space* Phoenix
R. L. GREEN *Into Other Worlds* Schumann
F. HOYLE *The Nature of the Universe* Blackwell
J. JEANS *The Mysterious Universe* C.U.P.
The Stars in their Courses C.U.P.
A. C. B. LOVELL *The Individual and the Universe* O.U.P.
R. A. LYTTLETON *The Modern Universe* Hodder & Stoughton
D. MOORE *Science in Fiction* Harrap

PERIODICALS

There are a few British SF periodicals, the best of which is probably *New Worlds*. SF stories also appear regularly in *Argosy*. The best known of the American ones devoted entirely to SF are *Galaxy* and *Astounding Science Fiction*.

EXERCISES

Pictures Don't Lie

1. What was the mistake everyone made about the aliens? Explain it in your own words.
2. How does the writer create the impression that there is something wrong with Nathen's calculations?
3. What is the importance of Jacob Luke in the story?
4. Imagine you are Bud and write an account of your arrival on Earth.

The Cold Equations

5. (a) 'It was a girl.' Why should this statement alter the pilot's attitude to the stowaway?
   (b) In what respect could the girl's upbringing be responsible for her predicament?
6. What question of morals is starkly presented in this story?
7. Make a brief summary of the plot and list the elements of the story which would be found only in SF. What, if anything, does the story gain from this background?

A Sound of Thunder

8. Explain in your own words why Travis and Lesperance are so insistent that no one should leave the metal path.
9. In the introduction it is suggested that time-travel involves certain 'philosophical difficulties.' What examples can you find in this story?
10. 'Scientists know not what they do.' By careful reference to relevant incidents, show that this is the theme of the story.
11. Pick out any twelve expressions which you would use to show that Ray Bradbury is a very sensuous writer.

He Walked Around the Horses

12. At what point in the story do you begin to suspect that the letters were not written in our world? Explain why the ending is so satisfactory.

13. Write a *brief* summary of the events of the story in chronological order.
14. Pick out some examples of humour from the story.
15. Show how the author alters his style to reflect the different characters of the letter writers.

Zero Hour

16. (a) When is the sinister element first introduced?
    (b) How is this sustained in the dialogue?
17. What, in your opinion, is the most important point that the author is making in this story?
18. Make a careful analysis of the plot and show how it develops towards a crisis.

The Crystal Egg

19. (a) How was the image in the Egg first observed and then improved?
    (b) What factors led the observers to conclude they were seeing Mars?
20. The description of Mars and the nature of the Egg are deliberately tantalizing. Why would it have detracted from the effect of the story if H. G. Wells had been more explicit about these subjects?
21. Write short character studies of Mr. and Mrs. Cave, and Mr. Wace. Explain the importance of any *one* of them in the story.

Dormant

22. (a) How is the sinister atmosphere created at the beginning of the story?
    (b) How are man's efforts made to look ineffective?
23. Explain in what way the end of this story is ironical.
24. Write a character study of Maynard.
25. Write an account of Iilah from information *given in the story*.

The Sea Raiders

26. List all the occasions when the Sea Raiders are sighted.
27. What information is given about their appearance and habits? How do all these 'facts' make us believe the Raiders are real?
28. What does Mr. Fison's adventure add to the account? Tell his story in your own words.

Dumb Show

29. (a) Outline the contrast which is drawn between the 'ill-matched pair,' Pauline and Mrs. Snowden.
    (b) How does the author use these two characters to reveal what has happened in the war?
30. Beginning ' "DON'T," screamed Mrs. Snowden's dumb card. I made a face at her and . . .' continue the story as though you are Pauline, but use your own words as far as possible.

The Nine Billion Names of God

31. 'There is a philosophical problem of some difficulty here, which I do not propose to discuss . . .' Why is the author deliberately vague about the 'man-made labels' which are the names of God?
32. What does the High Lama mean when he says to Church, 'It's nothing as trivial as *that*'?
33. Suggest some reasons why Wagner, Church and George all think the Tibetan Lamas are mad.
34. What differences can you find between the Westerners and the Lamas?

Panel Game

35. (a) What signs of material 'progress' can you find in the story?
    (b) Find some examples of parodies of 'high pressure' salesmanship?
36. What kind of humour is used in this story?
37. What is meant by pathos? What aspects of the story are pathetic rather than amusing?

The Man in Asbestos

38. Which parts of the story do you find particularly amusing? Why?
39. What 'improvements' on the twentieth century way of life have been made in the future?
40. In what ways does the Man in Asbestos find the narrator amusing or odd?
41. Write a commentary on the story bringing out its allegorical nature.